Labour Law in Latvia

Labour Law in Latvia

Third Edition

Ineta Tāre

This book was originally published as a monograph in the International Encyclopaedia of Laws/Labour Law and Industrial Relations.

Founding Editor: Roger Blanpain
General Editor: Frank Hendrickx
Volume Editor: Frank Hendrickx

Wolters Kluwer

Published by:
Kluwer Law International B.V.
PO Box 316
2400 AH Alphen aan den Rijn
The Netherlands
E-mail: international-sales@wolterskluwer.com
Website: lrus.wolterskluwer.com

Sold and distributed in North, Central and South America by:
Wolters Kluwer Legal & Regulatory U.S.
7201 McKinney Circle
Frederick, MD 21704
United States of America
Email: customer.service@wolterskluwer.com

Sold and distributed in all other countries by:
Air Business Subscriptions
Rockwood House
Haywards Heath
West Sussex
RH16 3DH
United Kingdom
Email: international-customerservice@wolterskluwer.com

ISBN 978-94-035-2292-0

e-Book: ISBN 978-94-035-2293-7
web-PDF: ISBN 978-94-035-2294-4

The Author

Ms Ineta Tāre works for the Ministry of Welfare of the Republic of Latvia. At present, she is the Director of the International Cooperation and EU Policy Department, where she is the Senior Official of the Ministry of Welfare in EU Affairs. Previously she has been Director of the Labour Department at the same Ministry, dealing with labour law, employment policy, industrial relations, health and safety at work, work-life balance.

Ms Ineta Tāre holds a Master's in Law and for several years has been guest Lecturer for students on the Human Resources Management Programme.

The Author

Table of Contents

Table of Contents

List of Abbreviations

CSB	Central Statistical Bureau
EC	European Community
ECHR	European Convention on Human Rights
EFA	European Free Alliance
EWC	European Works Council
EU	European Union
EU-15	EU Countries before 1 May 2004
EU-12	EU Countries which joined the EU on 1 May 2004 and on 1 January 2007
EURES	European Job Mobility Portal
GDP	Gross Domestic Product
GUE/NGL	European United Left/Nordic Green Left
HR	Human Resources
ILO	International Labour Organization
IMF	International Monetary Fund
JKP	The New Conservative Party
KPV LV	Political Party 'Who Owns the State'
LBAS	Free Trade Union Federation of Latvia
NATO	North Atlantic Treaty Organization
OECD	Organisation for Economic Co-operation and Development
OSCE	Organization for Security and Cooperation in Europe
SEA	State Employment Agency
SLI	State Labour Inspectorate
SME	Small and Medium-Sized Enterprise
SSIA	State Social Insurance Agency
TB	For Fatherland and Freedom
SD	Progressive Alliance of Socialists and Democrats
UN	United Nations
USSR	Union of Soviet Socialist Republics
ZZS	The Union of Greens and Farmers

List of Abbreviations

General Introduction

Chapter 1. General Background

§1. Geography, Location, Size and Boundaries

1. Latvia is a small country, the central country of the Baltic states (Estonia, Latvia, and Lithuania). On the world map, Latvia is to be found in north-eastern Europe, on the east coast of the Baltic Sea (the length of Latvia's Baltic coastline is 494 km). It is a part of the Balto-Scandinavian geographic region. Latvia covers an area of 64,559 km^2 or 24,937 mi^2. It borders Estonia to the north, Russia to the east, Lithuania and Belarus to the south, the Baltic Sea to the west. Most of the countryside is less than 100 metres above sea level; 57% of the country lies less than 100 metres above the sea level, 40.5% lies between 100 and 200 m, and 2.5% is above 200 m.

In Latvia, there are 2,300 lakes and 12,000 rivers, 17 of them longer than 100 km. The River Daugava is the longest river with a total length of 1,005 km; 352 km of the river lies in the territory of Latvia. Of the territory of Latvia, 45.4% is covered by woods. In summer the average temperature is 15.8°C, and in wintertime it is –4.5°C. There are approximately 120 days with precipitation per annum. In the capital city, Riga the highest registered temperature has reached 34.5°C and the lowest one at –34.9°C; it has been 35.1°C and –43.2°C in Daugavpils.

The country has a population of 1.91 million[1] and some thirty-one inhabitants per square kilometre (approximately 0.633 million inhabitants live in Riga, the capital of the Republic – 2,300 inhabitants per square kilometre; 33% of all population of Latvia – one of the highest). Other important cities include Daugavpils, an industrial centre in the south-east, on the Daugava River; Liepàja, an important port on the Baltic Sea; Jelgava, an industrial centre near Riga; Júrmala, a resort town on the Gulf of Riga; and Ventspils, another leading seaport. Numerous villages and small cities are located along the country's rivers, waterways, and coastal areas.

2. Latvia's society is multi-ethnic – more than 150 ethnicities are living in Latvia. Latvians are the indigenous people of Latvia, and the Finno-Ugric Livs (or Livonians) are the only indigenous minority. Latvia's present ethnic mix is mostly a result of massive post-war immigration, which resulted in a decline in the share of ethnic Latvians from 77% in 1935 to 52% in 1989, and 59.4% in 2010.

1. The Central Statistical Bureau of Latvia, http://www.csb.gov.lv; last visited 31 Dec. 2019.

Latvian is the official state language. As of 1 January 2019, the population of Latvia was as follows: 1,196,578 Latvians, 478,667 Russians, 61,429 Belorussians, 38,821 Ukrainians, 22,344 Poles, 43,069 Lithuanians and 67,885 other nationalities.[2] At the beginning of 2019, the population of Latvia was close to 2 million persons, 40% of whom were aged 50 and over. This age group comprised almost one-third of Latvia's working-age population.

§2. The Political System

3. By the Constitution, the sovereign power belongs to the people of Latvia. The political life of Latvia takes place in the framework of a parliamentary democratic republic, where the Prime Minister is the head of government, and a multi-party system.

The President of Latvia holds a primarily ceremonial role as head of State,[3] may request a re-examination of law, has a right to submit an application to the Constitutional Court requesting to initiate constitutional proceedings concerning the compatibility of legislation with the Constitution. The President of Latvia has a right to initiate dissolution of *Saeima* (a unicameral Parliament consisting of 100 members who are elected by proportional representation, with seats allocated to political parties which gain at least 5% of the popular vote).[4]

The former President of Latvia Mr Valdis Zatlers initiated the dissolution of the Parliament in an address to the nation on 28 May 2011 just before the presidential elections to be held on 2 June 2011. In his speech, broadcast live on public television and radio, the President of Latvia announced his decision to initiate the dissolution of the Parliament, based on Article 48 of the Latvian Constitution (*Satversme*), which stipulates that the President of Latvia has the right to propose the dissolution of the Parliament, which is to be followed by a national referendum within the next two months. According to the procedure, set in the Constitution of Latvia, if the referendum approves the Presidents of Latvia's move, the next general election also has to be organized within one to two months, and the new Parliament would then have a month to convene for its first session. Thus, the whole process should take no more than five months. The referendum on the dissolution of Latvia's Parliament took place on 23 July 2011 and the general elections on 17 September 2011.

The Latvian Constitution (*Satversme)* stipulates that the *Saeima* shall be elected in general, equal, and direct elections, by secret ballot based on proportional representations. The *Saeima* is composed of 100 members and generally elected for a term of four years. Since this election was not a regular one, the next *Saeima* had to be elected in three years, on 4 October 2014.[5]

The number of members from each district shall be proportional to the number of electors in each district. The Central Election Commission determines the number

2. The Central Statistical Bureau of Latvia, http://www.csb.gov.lv, last visited 31 Dec. 2019.
3. Official homepage of Latvian State President, http://www.president.lv/, last visited 31 Dec. 2019.
4. The Parliament (*Saeima*), http://www.saeima.lv/english, last visited 31 Dec. 2019.
5. The Central Election Commission, last visited 1 Dec. 2019.

of seats in the Saeima in proportion to the number of voters in a constituency as stated four months before Election Day according to the data provided by the Population Register. If the *Saeima* elections take place according to Article 48 of the Constitution, the number of seats is decided on the day when the elections are announced. Voters residing in foreign countries are included among voters of the Riga constituency.

Legislative power is vested in both the Government and Parliament, the *Saeima*. Legally the *Saeima* has several tools for control over the Cabinet of Ministers, including parliamentary questions, requests, parliamentary investigatory committees, and votes of non-confidence:

- The *Saeima* may express non-confidence in the Prime Minister or in particular ministers.
- No fewer than five members of Parliament may submit questions to the Prime Minister, his/her deputies, ministers, state ministers, and the President of the Bank of Latvia in order to clarify issues within the competence of the above officials. Answers may be presented either orally or in written form,
- No fewer than ten members of Parliament may submit a request. Requests are submitted either to the Presidium of the *Saeima* or – between sittings – to the Chancellery of the *Saeima*. Then the Committee of Petitions reviews the requests and finds whether each particular request is acceptable, partly acceptable or unacceptable. Finally, the *Saeima* decides whether to accept or reject a request. If a request is accepted, it is sent to the Prime Minister or another relevant official. Answers are to be submitted within seven days and are then debated in the Parliament,
- The *Saeima* must set up parliamentary investigatory commissions for particular issues if no less than one-third of *Saeima* members request so.

4. Executive power in Latvia is exercised by the government. The Cabinet of Ministers is the highest executive body of the country.[6] The Cabinet of Ministers is formed by a person invited by the President of Latvia. The Cabinet of Ministers consists of the Prime Minister and other ministers appointed by the Prime Minister. The Prime Minister may invite one Deputy Prime Minister as a member of the Cabinet of Ministers and one or more ministers for special assignments. The Cabinet of Ministers determines the duties of the Deputy Prime Minister and the ministers for special assignments. The Prime Minister may also appoint a state minister. In addition to his direct responsibilities, the Prime Minister may permanently lead the work of one ministry. The Cabinet of Ministers starts exercising its duties after receiving a confidence vote by the *Saeima*. Ministers and state ministers appointed by the Prime Minister at a later stage should receive a special confidence vote by the *Saeima*.

If the *Saeima* passes a no-confidence vote on the Prime Minister, the whole Cabinet must resign. If a minister receives a non-confidence vote, he/she must resign, and the Prime Minister should invite another person to take over the responsibilities. The *Saeima* expresses its non-confidence to all the Cabinet by adopting a decision or by rejecting the annual state budget submitted by the Cabinet.

6. Law on the Structure of Cabinet of Ministers, http://www.mk.gov.lv, last visited 1 Dec. 2019.

The Prime Minister must notify the President of Latvia, and the Chairperson of the *Saeima* regarding the resignation of Cabinet; the latter should present this notification at the next sitting of the *Saeima*.

The Prime Minister or individual ministers and state ministers who have resigned from office either with or without an expression of non-confidence from the *Saeima*, should continue to fulfil their duties of the office unless the *Saeima* has decided otherwise and has appointed persons to temporarily assume these offices until a successor is appointed.

If the Prime Minister requests the resignation of a minister or a state minister, the state minister should resign even without a no-confidence vote by the *Saeima*. If one or several ministers resign, the Prime Minister himself/herself may temporarily take over their responsibilities or assign them to other ministers. The Prime Minister should invite other persons to replace the resigned ministers. The invited persons should take the office of a minister only after receiving a confidence vote by the *Saeima*.

The Cabinet of Ministers has legislative rights, and public institutions are subject to the authority of the Cabinet of Ministers. The Cabinet of Ministers has rights to appoint a broad range of civil servants or approve their status, discusses, or decides on all issues within its scope of competence according to the *Satversme* and other laws.

5. In Latvia, there exists a national human rights institution – the Ombudsman's Office – established initially in 1995 as the National Human Rights Office in compliance with the UN Paris Principles.[7] The Ombudsman fulfils the following functions:

(a) to promote the protection of the human rights of a private individual;
(b) to promote compliance with the principles of equal treatment and prevention of any discrimination;
(c) to evaluate and promote compliance with the principles of good governance in the state administration;
(d) to discover deficiencies in the legislation and the application thereof regarding the issues related to the observance of human rights and the principle of good governance, as well as to promote the rectification of such deficiencies;
(e) to promote the public awareness and understanding of human rights, of the mechanisms for the protection of such rights and the activities of the Ombudsman.

During 2018 there were 1,716 written submissions for the Ombudsman; 280 verification procedures have been completed, and 3,030 responses have been prepared; 6,861 consultations have been provided, forty-five cases were initiated, and forty-three cases have been completed.

Priorities for 2018 were:

7. http://www.tiesibsargs.lv/eng/, last visited 1 Dec. 2019.

(1) safeguarding of children's rights in psycho-neurological hospitals and orphanages (where children are in a particularly vulnerable situation compared to children in families); and
(2) protecting the rights of seniors in nursing homes for the elderly.

The visits included: (1) Children's Psychoneurological Hospitals, (2) orphanages, (3) state social care centres in which persons with mental disabilities are placed, (4) nursing homes for the elderly, (5) authorities, etc.

6. The judicial branch is independent of the executive and the legislature. Judicial power under the Law on Judicial Power is vested in the courts.[8]

There is a three-level court system in Latvia.

Court cases are heard by district (city) courts, regional courts and the Supreme Court, and, as stated in Article 82 of the Constitution of Latvia,[9] in the event of war or a state of emergency, also by military courts. Judges should be independent and subject only to law. The first level of the judicial system comprises thirty-three district (city) courts, including the administrative district court, as the courts of the first instance for civil, criminal and administrative cases.

Regional courts can be both courts of the first instance and courts of appeal. A regional court is the court of the first instance where procedural legislation lays down that a specific case must be heard in a regional court at first instance. This usually applies to cases which are more complex or have a greater scope. Regional courts operate as courts of appeal for civil, criminal and administrative cases that have been heard in a district (municipal) court or by a sole judge. There are six regional courts in Latvia: the Riga Regional Court, the Kurzeme Regional Court, the Latgale Regional Court, the Vidzeme Regional Court, the Zemgale Regional Court and the Regional Administrative Court.

The Supreme Court of the Republic of Latvia (third level) is composed of the Senate and two Court Chambers: the Civil Chamber and the Criminal Chamber. The Senate is made up of four departments: the Department of Civil Cases, the Department of Criminal Cases, the Department of Administrative Cases and the Department of Disciplinary Cases. The Judgments of the Supreme Court are final. By the law, the Supreme Court reviews appeals in its capacity as the court of the second instance (*de novo* review) and as the court of the third instance (cassation review). All judges are appointed by the *Saeima* at the recommendation of the Minister of Justice (judges of the Supreme Court – at the recommendation of the Chairman of the Supreme Court). The *Saeima* has determined that the Supreme Court should have forty-eight judges. Latvia's judicial system has been reorganized – on 31 December 2014, the Chamber of Criminal Cases was abolished, and the Chamber of Civil Cases was active until 31 December 2016.[10] Hereinafter the Supreme Courts are the cassation instance only.

8. Law on Judicial Power, 15 Dec. 1992, http://www.vvc.gov.lv, last visited 1 Dec. 2019.
9. *Latvijas Republikas Satversme*, http://www.saeima.lv, last visited 1 Dec. 2019.
10. www.at.gov.lv, Book on History of the Chamber of Civil Cases, last visited 1 Dec. 2019.

The Constitutional Court (*Satversmes tiesa*) is not a part of the general court system. It is an independent court authority – a special court, which reviews cases concerning the compliance of laws with the Constitution of Latvia (*Satversme*), as well as other matters as defined by law. The Constitutional Court considers issues of compliance of laws and regulations with the Constitution.

The Constitutional Court of Latvia shall adjudicate cases regarding: (a) compliance of laws with the Constitution; (b) compliance of international agreements signed or entered into by Latvia (also until the confirmation of the relevant agreements in the *Saeima*) with the Constitution; (c) compliance of other regulatory enactments or parts thereof with the norms (acts) of a higher legal force; (d) compliance of other acts of the *Saeima*, the Cabinet, the President, the Speaker of the *Saeima* and the Prime Minister, except for administrative acts, with law; (e) compliance with law of such an order with which a Minister authorized by the Cabinet has suspended a decision taken by a local government council; and (f) compliance of Latvian national legal norms with those international agreements entered into by Latvia that is not in conflict with the Constitution. The Constitutional Court is not entitled to bring actions on its initiative; it hears cases only upon application by persons specified under the legislation. This court has ruled on issues of policy, for example, overturning government policy on social security provisions, ruling on governmental non-compliance with access to information legislation. The Constitutional Court has the right to declare laws or other enactments or parts thereof invalid.

The Act on the Constitutional Court[11] lays down that claims may be brought before the Constitutional Court by the President of Latvia, the *Saeima,* at least twenty parliamentary deputies, the Cabinet of Ministers, the Prosecutor General, the State Audit Office, the Ombudsman's Office and local authorities (councils); applications may also be made by courts of general jurisdiction hearing civil, criminal or administrative cases, land registry department judges registering immovable property or recording rights associated with such property in the land registry, and any natural or legal person whose fundamental rights as laid down in the Constitution have been infringed.

The Constitutional Court consists of seven judges who are each elected by the Saeima for a ten-year term. Judgments of the Constitutional Court are final and non-appealable. They enter into force upon their promulgation and are binding on all state and local government institutions, authorities, and officials, including the courts, and also on natural and legal persons. Any legislative provision which the Constitutional Court has found not to be in compliance with another legislative provision with higher legal force is considered invalid from the day on which the Constitutional Court's judgment is published unless otherwise specified by the Constitutional Court. Where the Constitutional Court has found that an international agreement signed or concluded by Latvia does not comply with the Constitution, the Cabinet is immediately required to draft amendments to the agreement in question, to denounce the agreement, to suspend its application or to revoke adherence to the agreement.

11. http://www.satv.tiesa.gov.lv/?lang=2&mid=9, last visited 1 Dec. 2019.

7. In 1989 the Latvian Supreme Soviet ended the Communist Party's political monopoly, and there was a rise in a number of independent political parties and the opportunities for free elections, that had not been possible in Latvia since 1940. The results of the first free election (18 March 1990) saw only 15 of the 201 pro-Soviet deputies re-elected. Approximately two-thirds of the new members belonged to the Popular Front of Latvia (LTF), a pro-independence party (formed in 1988).

On 4 May 1990, the Supreme Council adopted a declaration on the restoration of independence of the Republic of Latvia,[12] declared Soviet annexation illegal, and partly reintroduced the 1922 Constitution (*Satversme*), in fact, restored the Republic of Latvia founded on 18 November 1918.

On 21 August 1991, during the 'Soviet coup' in Moscow, Latvia declared full independence but failed to enact all components of the 4 May 1990 Declaration because of questions about the legitimacy of the new government and whether amendments to the 1922 Constitution should be permitted.

8. Since 1991 the political scene in Latvia has been characterized by change and the emergence of new political parties, especially prior general or municipal elections (lately also elections for the European Parliament) before election campaigns.[13] Before the *Saeima* general election in 2018, there were sixteen parties and electoral coalitions. This is the largest number of lists since 2006 with nineteen lists. From 2010 to 2014 (there was an extraordinary election in 2011 after the *Saeima* was dismissed by the then President Valdis Zatlers) the number of lists was steady at thirteen.[14] However, many of them barely met the minimum membership requirement and functioned at a local level rather than nationally. Some parties were created to represent a specific group, others – as a result of commonly shared goals and values. Still, others serve as a platform for the politically ambitious. The diverse origins of the parties help to explain why their policies and actions tend to reflect a 'mixed' orientation that is not grounded consistently in the traditional doctrines of either the political right or left.

9. Distribution of parties: Latvia has a multi-party system, where no one party often has a chance of gaining power alone, and parties must work with each other to form coalition governments.

The following political parties were represented in the *Saeima* (after the elections of 2018):

– Social Democratic Party 'Harmony' – twenty-two MPs and two MEPs. Since the 2014 general elections, the Concord parliamentary group has held twenty-four seats in the *Saeima* and continues to be the main opposition party. The 2019 election for the European Parliament ensured two seats (S&D).

12. http://www.likumi.lv/doc.php?id=75539, last visited 31 Dec. 2019.
13. http://providus.lv/article_files/3555/original/Political_Ideologies_and_the_EU_in_Latvia's_Representative_Democracy.pdf?1557753750, last visited 15 Dec. 2019.
14. https://en.rebaltica.lv/2018/08/who-is-who-in-upcoming-latvian-parliamentary-elections/, last visited 15 Dec. 2019.

– The centre-right party 'New Unity' – 8 MPs and 2 MEPs. The party held the office of Prime Minister in several consecutive coalition governments and is currently a member of the government coalition. The Latvian Prime Minister is Mr A.K. Karins, Member of the 'New Unity'. The 2019 election for the European Parliament ensured two seats (EPP).
– The Union of Greens and Farmers (ZZS).[15] In the last general election 2018 ZZS gained ten seats in *Saeima.*
– The National Alliance,[16] an alliance of the national conservative party For Fatherland and Freedom/LNNK and the far-right All for Latvia! was formed for the *Saeima* elections in 2010. The National Alliance was transformed into the united party in 2011. The Party has been a member of several government coalitions, including the current one. According to the results of the 2018 general elections, the National Alliance parliamentary group has twelve seats in the *Saeima.* In 2019 elections for the European Parliament the National Alliance won two seats.
– Newly established political party 'Who Owns the State?' (KPV LV).[17] KPV LV received the second largest number of votes (14.25%) among the parties that participated in the 2018 Latvian parliamentary election and earned sixteen seats in the thirteenth Saeima. The party is currently a member of the government coalition.
– The New Conservative Party (JKP[18]) is a conservative political party in Latvia, has been founded in 2014. The 2018 election for the Latvian Parliament ensured sixteen seats and membership in the government coalition.
– Development/For! is a liberal, pro-European political alliance[19] in Latvia, made of three political parties. After the 2018 Latvian parliamentary election, it is the fourth largest political group in the Saeima (thirteen seats). It takes part in the government coalition and has won one seat at the European Parliament.

Latvia is a party to major international agreements laying the basis for democratic elections. By signing the Coalition agreement, the parties constituting the government promised to reduce the dependence of Latvian political parties on private donations by increasing the state budget funding to the average level of the Baltic States. The State has been paying the parties since 2012.

10. The Republic of Latvia is composed of the four historical regions of Vidzeme, Kurzeme, Latgale and Zemgale and from 1 July 2009 is divided into 110 local governments and nine republican cities – Riga, Jūrmala, Valmiera, Jelgava, Ventspils, Daugavpils, Rēzekne, Liepàja and Jēkabpils.

The aim of the administrative-territorial reform that started 1992 was to reduce the number of administrative levels and to increase the capacity of local administrative units. Five administrative units, one per each of five planning regions (Rīga, Vidzeme, Kurzeme, Zemgale and Latgale), have been established. The planning

15. http://www.zzs.lv, last visited 1 Dec. 2019.
16. http://www.nacionalaapvieniba, last visited 1 Dec. 2019.
17. https://kampiedervalsts.com/, last visited 1 Dec. 2019.
18. https://konservativie.lv/, last visited 1 Dec. 2019.
19. https://attistibaipar.lv/, last visited 1 Dec. 2019.

regions ensure the planning and co-ordination of regional development and cooperation between local government and other state administrative institutions. The planning regions of Latvia are not administrative-territorial divisions.

Local authorities benefit from significant autonomy from the central government, as guaranteed by the Law on Local Government. They operate independently within the framework of their competencies and legislation and have their property, separate from the property of the state. All local authorities have equal competencies, except for Riga, which has broader competencies and special functions, reflecting its status as the capital city. Local authorities are elected for a term of four years by direct universal elections, under proportional representation.

The number of municipalities in Latvia will be reduced from 119 to 36 until 2021. The plan foresees the creation of much larger and economically stronger municipalities around Latvia's largest cities and development centres, which would facilitate the provision of high-quality municipal services.[20]

11. Participation in global and regional organizations, especially membership of the EU, North Atlantic Treaty Organization (NATO), the International Monetary Fund (IMF) and other organizations (such as the Council of Europe and the Organization for Security and Cooperation in Europe (OSCE)) is becoming increasingly important for Latvia. Such participation enables Latvia to meet new challenges and to contribute to the resolution of specific problems, while also representing the country's national interests in global politics.

Latvia joined the NATO on 29 March 2004, and the European Union on 1 May 2004. Latvia has been a participating in the OSCE since 1991 and to the Council of Europe since 1995.[21]

From 1 January 2014, Latvia has joined Euro-zone countries, by introducing the Euro currency.[22] On 1 July 2016 Latvia deposited its instrument of accession to the Organisation for Economic Co-operation and Development (OECD) Convention, thereby becoming a full member of the OECD.

Latvia has acceded to the major UN human rights instruments and has established constructive cooperation with various treaty bodies. Latvia has led the Presidency of the Council of the European Union in the first half of 2015.

§3. Population and Employment Statistics

12. Latvia has historically had an ethnic Latvian majority speaking Latvian, but also large minority populations (especially in urban centres) speaking different languages.[23] Russian is the most widespread minority language in Latvia; 37% of the population are native Russian speakers.

20. The Ministry of Environmental Protection and Regional Development of the Republic of Latvia, http://www.varam.gov.lv, last visited 15 Dec. 2019.
21. The Ministry of Foreign Affairs of the Republic of Latvia, http://www.mfa.gov.lv, last visited 15 Dec. 2019.
22. http://www.eiro.lv/eng/, last visited 1 Dec. 2019.
23. OECD Reviews of Labour Market and Social Policies: Latvia; 2016, p. 14.

The data of the Population Register of Latvia show that on 1 July 2019, Latvian citizens constitute 1,770,984 persons,[24] 220,491 persons are Latvian non-citizens. Non-citizens are a special category of persons defined by the Law on the Status of those Former USSR Citizens who are not Citizens of Latvia or Any Other State[25] as persons who resided in Latvia on 1 July 1991, and have not obtained the citizenship of any other country. This special status was established in 1995 as a temporary status for former USSR citizens and their descendants living in the Republic of Latvia who do not have Latvian or any other state's citizenship. In relation to such individuals, Latvia has undertaken particular obligations – it guarantees *ex lege* residence in Latvia, consular protection abroad, the right to return to Latvia and the right no to be extradited from Latvia. However, the rights of citizens and non-citizens differ to some extent, for example, regarding voting rights at local, national and European election.

The Latvian Constitution (*Satversme*) stipulates that 'persons belonging to ethnic minorities have the right to preserve and develop their language and their ethnic and cultural identity'. All Latvia's permanent residents are guaranteed the right to establish their own state facilitated national societies, unions and associations. It should be mentioned that every non-citizen has the right to acquire Latvian citizenship through naturalization via recognition of citizenship, registration of citizen's status, naturalization and restoration of citizenship.[26]

Since the beginning of naturalization process on 1 February 1995, 140,765 persons have been naturalized: in 1995 – 984; in 1996 – 3,016; in 1997 – 2,992; in 1998 – 4,439; in 1999 – 12,427; in 2000 – 14,900; in 2001 – 10,637, in 2002 – 9844; in 2003 – 10,049; in 2004 – 16,064; in 2005 – 19,169; in 2006 – 16,439; in 2007 – 6,826; in 2008 – 3,004; in 2009 – 2,080; in 2010 – 2,336; in 2011 – 2,467; in 2012 – 2,213; in 2013 – 1,732; in 2014 – 939; in 2015 – 971, in 2016 – 987, in 2017 – 915, in 2018 – 930, in 2019 – 739.

Latvia has achieved considerable progress in the facilitation of the naturalization process by reducing the number of non-citizens.[27] From 1 January 2020, children born in Latvia will receive either Latvian citizenship or citizenship of another country if both parents agree on that other citizenship. The default will be Latvian citizenship for all children born to Latvia-resident parents. If the child is born outside Latvia or one of the parents is a citizen of another country, the parents will have to submit an application and documents certifying that the child is not and has not been a citizen of any other country in order to be recognized as a Latvian citizen.

24. http://www.pmlp.gov.lv, last, last visited 15 Dec. 2019.
25. http://www.vvc.gov.lv/export/sites/default/docs/LRTA/Likumi/On_the_Status_of_those_Former_U.S.S.R._Citizens_.doc, last visited 15 Dec. 2019.
26. http://www.pmlp.gov.lv/en/home/citizenship/naturalization/, last visited 15 Dec. 2019.
27. In 1995, in parallel with the status of citizen of Latvia, the status of non-citizen of Latvia was established as special temporary status to citizens of former USSR and their descendants who live in the Republic of Latvia and who do not have the citizenship of Latvia or any other country. Non-citizens of Latvia cannot be considered stateless persons under the Convention Relating to the Status of Stateless Persons of 1954 because the non-citizens have much more extensive rights.

I. Labour Market

13. Rapid growth was observed in Latvia from 2004 to 2007 when GDP grew annually by 11% on average. Such high growth rates were mainly ensured by the domestic demand, which was based mostly on the substantial inflow of foreign capital. Both private consumption and investment rose considerably. Export increase played a less significant role in the growth and asset prices boomed. Average wage growth reached 20% to 30% annually, far outrunning productivity.

The economy still remains a preoccupation for Latvians, after Latvia experienced one of the worst economic recessions in the EU, with a GDP contraction of –25% on accumulated bases in 2008–2009.[28] Since independence was restored, the highest level of unemployment was recorded in 1996 at 20.5%. In comparison, this figure stood at just 0.5% of the active population in 1990. After Latvia's accession to the EU, its economy had been growing rapidly – at about 10% a year up until 2008. The availability of credit had stimulated an increase in domestic demand that had been tending to a reduction in unemployment levels. In 2004, the level of unemployment stood at 10.4% and continued to decline in 2005 (8.7%), 2006 (6.8%) and 2007 (4.4%). However, in 2008, all of the country's economic sectors experienced a decline in growth, i.e., GDP fell by 4.6% in 2008.[29]

The agreed budget deficit benchmark for 2009 was 10% of GDP, to be gradually reduced to 8.5% in 2010 and finally to 3% by 2012. The Latvian government has obtained EUR 7.5 billion financial rescue package from the IMF, the European Commission, the World Bank, the European Reconstruction and Development Bank and several regional countries (Nordic countries). Latvia returned to strong economic growth in 2011 and 2012 after a severe downturn and a strict austerity programme. In late 2012, Latvia even repaid to the IMF full amount of credit, several years early.

14. The government opted for a dramatic fiscal tightening in 2008–2010, including reduction of social security benefits, significant tax hikes and further staff, wage, and guaranties cuts in the public sector. Latvia undertook significant consolidation measures in 2009–2012 (around 3% of GDP per year). The general government deficit reached -7.7% of GDP in 2010 and -4.5% of GDP in 2011. More consolidation measures followed in 2012 to bring down the deficit below 3% of GDP in order to prepare to join the Euro-zone from 1 January 2014.

The general government gross debt increased rapidly from 9% of GDP in 2007 to 44.7% of GDP in 2010; in 2012 it fell until 36% of GDP and in May 2013 stood at 35.2% of the forecast GDP 2013. Since 2011, output recovery in Latvia has been among the fastest in the European Union but in 2017 GDP returned to the pre-crisis level.[30]

---

28. The Ministry of Welfare, Report on Labour Market, http://www.lm.gov.lv, last visited 15 Dec. 2019.
29. The Ministry of Economics of the Republic of Latvia, http://www.em.gov.lv, last visited 15 Dec. 2019.
30. OECD Reviews of Labour Market and Social Policies: Latvia, 2016.

Latvia's GDP growth remained moderate through-out 2017–2018, which, given the external environment, can be considered a satisfactory result. In view of the persistently tense geopolitical situation, worsening of the global economic growth forecasts and those of a part of the trade partners, and the weak investment dynamics, GDP forecasts have been revised downwards.[31] Throughout the last years, private consumption was supported by a rather steep acceleration of real net wages. Amid ongoing strengthening of purchasing power of the working population and stable consumer sentiment, private consumption is expected to be the driver of growth also in next years.

15. According to the reports by the Bank of Latvia,[32] the current financial indicators show that the country has fully regained its ability to compete in terms of cost competitiveness. Likewise, the increase in exports was among the fastest in the EU, and Latvia is regaining its market share in the world at large.

Starting from the second quarter of 2010 in Latvia, there was the most rapid employment growth in the EU. By the end of 2010, the unemployment rate had stabilized, with this tendency remaining unchanged also in the following years. It indicates that the majority of companies have adopted necessary decisions in respect of the number of employees. Thus, the substantial changes in the labour market are not predicted.[33]

16. In other words, Latvia has gone back on track both financially and economically. In 2018, Latvia's external demand posted a more moderate increase than a year ago on account of the slowdown observed in the economic growth globally, in the euro area, as well as in Latvia's major trade partners. The deteriorating economic sentiment in the euro area and escalating trade tensions between the US and China, along with a slowdown in international trade dynamics and concerns about the mounting protectionism risks, were the main constraints to more rapid economic growth in the euro area. Overall, growth is forecast to reach 2.6% in 2020 and increase slightly to 2.7% in 2021.

Confidence indicators in the industry, retail trade, services, construction and consumer sectors have all demonstrated improved confidence since early- to mid-2009. Domestic demand is increasingly becoming the main driver of the GDP growth.

Labour demand continued to expand during the past years. With more people entering the labour market, both participation rate and employment increased. Both participation and employment rates reached their historical highs. A growing number of formerly economically inactive persons are joining the labour market and the number of previously discouraged persons is declining. The number of long-term unemployed returning to the labour market is also increasing. Unemployment continued to shrink gradually and fell to the lowest level of the last eleven years (2018 – 7.4% of the economically active population).[34] Results of the LSF conducted by the Central Statistical Bureau show that 72.8 thousand people were unemployed in

31. The Bank of Latvia, http://www.bank.lv, last visited 15 Dec. 2019.
32. The Bank of Latvia, http://www.bank.lv/en/publications, last visited 15 Dec. 2019.
33. The Ministry of Welfare, Report on Labour Market, http://www.lm.gov.lv, last visited 15 Dec. 2019.
34. The Bank of Latvia, http://www.bank.lv, last visited 15 Dec. 2019.

2018. Compared to 2017, number of unemployed persons dropped by 12.6 thousand or 14.8%. Unemployment rate among females still was lower than among males – 6.4% and 8.4%, respectively. Since the third quarter of 2008, Latvian unemployment rate exceeds the European Union (EU) average. In 2018, youth unemployment rate constituted 12.2%. From 2013 to 2016, Latvian youth unemployment rate was lower than the EU average. The number of long-term unemployed persons (those who cannot find work for twelve months or more) is gradually reducing, and in 2018 it constituted 30.3 thousand persons (Figure 1).[35]

Figure 1 Unemployment Rate in the Baltic States and the European Union by Quarter (as %)

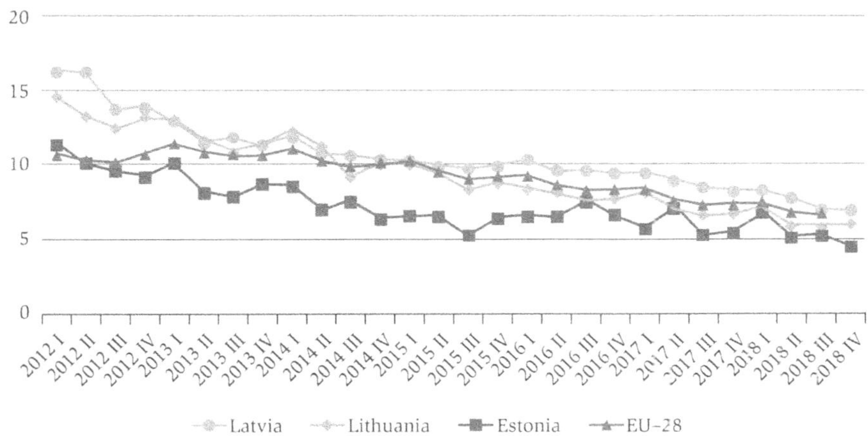

Source: Eurostat database, data on the Fourth Quarter of 2018 – Labour Force Surverys of Latvia, Lithuania and Estonia.

Table 1 Employment Statistics in Latvia

	2018
Unemployment rate (%)	7.4
Registered unemployment, end of period (numbers)	59,588
Employment rate (%)	64.5
Men	67.6
Women	61.7

Source: Central Statistical Bureau.

35. http://www.csb.gov.lv, last visited 15 Dec. 2019.

Given the declining size of the working-age population, economic growth is expected to depend on productivity increases rather than on rising employment also in the future. The overall rise in wages was supported by productivity gains and growing labour demand, the raising of the minimum wage and commitment to increasing wages in individual sectors (healthcare, education). Nominal wages grew by 7.6% in 2018. Wages rose in both the private and public sectors. The rising income increased well-being. However, higher productivity played an ever more important role in maintaining competitiveness.[36]

Monthly average gross wage and salary for full-time employment in 2018 was EUR 1,004, with its annual rise by 8.4%. Wages have been increasing at a steady pace for some time now with the average wage growth over the past five years, reaching 7.9%, substantially above the EU average of 1.6%. Starting from 1 January 2018 the minimum monthly wage in Latvia is EUR 430, up from EUR 380. Data of the Central Statistical Bureau (CSB) show that in 2018 the average gross wages and salaries for full-time work in Latvia comprised EUR 1,004. Compared to 2017, average wages and salaries rose by EUR 78 or 8.4%, moreover in all economic activities. Average net wages and salaries (calculated based on the labour taxes applicable to the workplace) comprised EUR 742 or 73.9% of the gross earnings. Over the year, net wages and salaries increased by 9.9%, showing 1.5 percentage points higher rise than that in the wages and salaries before taxes. Considering the consumer price growth of 2.5% in 2018, the real increase in wages and salaries comprised 7.2%. Compared to 2017, in 2018 rise in the minimum wage from EUR 380 to EUR 430 or by 13.2%, the introduction of progressive income tax, as well as changes in the size of differentiated untaxable minimum influenced changes in the average wages and salaries. The mandatory social insurance contributions paid by employees went up by 0.5 percentage points.

The pace of remuneration growth remains high and, in the long run, could affect the competitiveness of Latvia's goods and services. The overall increase in labour costs is lowering cost competitiveness for businesses. Thus, competing in external markets with lower production costs alone becomes increasingly more difficult as the production costs increase along with the rising wages.

Table 2 sets out the average monthly gross and net wages in Latvia and their growth rates, together with the real wage index, for each of the years ended 31 December 2013, 2014, 2015, 2016, 2017 and 2018.

Table 2 Wages in Latvia

	Year Ended 31 December					
	2013	*2014*	*2015*	*2016*	*2017*	*2018*
Average monthly gross wages[1] (EUR)	783	834	883	927	998	1,007
Gross growth (%)	(3.5)	4.4	3.7	4.6	6.8	6.8

36. http://www.bank.lv, last visited 15 Dec. 2019.

	Year Ended 31 December					
	2013	*2014*	*2015*	*2016*	*2017*	*2018*
Average monthly net wages[2] (EUR)	554	599	640	668	715	786
Consumer price index	100.0	100.6	100.2	100.1	102.9	102.5
Real wage index (% of previous year)	105.6	108.0	107.4	104.6	104.0	107.2

Source: CSB.

Notes

1. Total, excluding private sector enterprises with number of employees <50.

2. Total, excluding private sector enterprises with number of employees <50.

Employees by Monthly Net Wages and Salaries in the Main Job (as %)

	2017	*2018*	*2018*			
			Q1	*Q2*	*Q3*	*Q4*
Employees	**100.0**	**100.0**	**100.0**	**100.0**	**100.0**	**100.0**
up to EUR 450.00	39.2	30.5	34.9	30.6	28.9	27.7
employees receiving minimum monthly wage or less	19.1	16.9	20.5	17.4	15.3	14.3
EUR 450.01–700.00	32.4	34.4	33.7	34.9	33.5	35.6
EUR 700.01–1,400.00	20.2	25.7	22.6	25.3	27.1	27.9
EUR 1,400.01 and more	3.4	4.1	4.3	3.6	4.2	4.3
was not calculated or paid	2.7	2.6	1.6	3.0	3.3	2.3
not specified	2.1	2.7	2.9	2.6	3.0	2.2

Source: CSB.

17. The labour market has suffered due to the global financial crisis in 2008–2011 more severely than expected, beyond the European Commission's, IMF's and World Bank's forecasts of 10.4%. The unemployment rate in Latvia has been continuously growing since 2008 (from 6.9%), reaching its highest point in March 2010, with 20.4% of the economically active population lacking jobs. It was the second-highest rate in the EU, more than 153,000 persons. Youth unemployment almost tripled and was above 29% in June 2009.

Reflecting Latvia's emergence from recession, from 2010, the male employment rate has increased faster than the female employment rate and was 69.9% in 2015 compared to the female employment rate of 66.4%.

Female unemployment, according to Labour Force Survey data in 2010, was around 16.6%, while male unemployment was 23%. From 2010 to 2015, the total unemployment rate decreased from 19.8% to 10.1%. In 2015, male unemployment was 11.4%, while unemployment for women was 8.8%.

18. The largest share of unemployed persons is low-qualified labour force with a low education level. Disparities due to education level were pronounced: it is harder for the less educated to find a job. For instance, at the end of 2017, the job-seekers' ratio of university-educated people was several times smaller than the respective proportion of individuals with elementary education. Moreover, better-educated employees were paid higher wages.

The number of job vacancies increased slowly, and employment expectations of businesses remained neutral testifying that the economy neither displayed any signs of labour shortage nor anticipated it shortly. Besides, the business trend survey data suggest that the share of businesses referring to labour shortages as an essential obstacle to doing business is stable and moderate; hence there are no grounds to expect steeply rising unit labour costs. For the last years, many companies always referred to labour shortages as such an obstacle. It is likely that the employment indicators will be growing for the near future, and will depend on the employees' capabilities of acquiring additional knowledge and skills, getting educated in accordance with the market requirements, as employers in Latvia demand more qualified staff.

Table 3 shows annual average employment by sector in Latvia in 2013, 2014, 2015, 2016, 2017 and 2018.

Table 3 Latvian Employment Figures by Sector (1,000 Persons)

	2013	*2014*	*2015*	*2016*	*2017*	*2018*
Agriculture, forestry and fishing	71.9	66.3	71.1	71.9	66.3	71.1
Mining and quarrying	2.8	3.7	3.9	2.8	3.7	3.9
Manufacturing	125.7	118.8	116.3	125.7	118.8	116.3
Electricity, gas, steam and air conditioning supply	11.6	10.0	12.6	11.6	10.0	12.6
Water supply; sewage, waste management and remediation activities	6.2	5.2	7.1	6.2	5.2	7.1
Construction	67.3	73.2	71.9	67.3	73.2	71.9

	2013	*2014*	*2015*	*2016*	*2017*	*2018*
Wholesale and retail trade; repair services	133.4	132.3	128.9	133.4	132.3	128.9
Transportation and storage	77.3	84.8	85.3	77.3	84.8	85.3
Accommodation and food service activities	26.5	29.3	30.4	26.5	29.3	30.4
Information and communication	24.3	26.3	26.0	26.7	28.1	30.5
Financial and insurance activities	21.0	17.9	20.6	16.3	16.3	15.8
Real estate activities	22.7	20.7	20.7	19.9	20.3	20.8
Professional, scientific and technical activities	34.4	36.1	36.2	33.4	32.9	33.0
Administrative and support service activities	24.6	24.3	24.8	29.6	30.5	31.4
Public administration and defence; compulsory social security	61.3	58.6	59.1	56.5	57.2	57.4
Education	94.6	85.1	83.4	84.5	84.0	83.6
Human health and social work activities	47.7	52.0	55.8	49.5	50.4	51.0
Arts, entertainment and recreation	21.5	22.4	22.4	19.3	19.3	19.5
Other service activities	8.7	8.6	9.1	9.4	8.6	8.3
Activities of households as employers; undifferentiated goods and services producing activities of households for own use	N/A	N/A	N/A	N/A	N/A	N/A

Source: CSB; Age 15 to 64.

Based on CSB figures, 64.5% of Latvia population aged 15–74 were employed in 2018. Compared to 2017, employment rate grew by 1.6 percentage points and the number of employed persons by 14.6 thousand.

The most notable rise in the number of employed persons was recorded in construction, wholesale and retail trade, repair of motor vehicles and motorcycles, as well as administrative and support service activities.

19. Youth unemployment increased dramatically because of the crisis. Across the EU, it reached an average of more than 23%, and it was as high as 56% in some Member States. Young people were twice as likely to be unemployed as the adult population. Faced with such unacceptably high levels, the European Commission has been mobilizing its policies and instruments.[37] In December 2011, it presented a 'Youth Opportunities Initiative' setting out measures to drive down youth unemployment.

At the informal European Council meeting of 30 January 2012, as part of its 'Youth Opportunities Initiative', the European Commission called on the Member States to develop and implement comprehensive initiatives for youth employment, education and skills, and to develop youth jobs plans within their national reform programmes. It is mainly supporting young people who are not in education, employment, or training (NEETs), including long-term unemployed youngsters or those not registered as jobseekers.

The Commission also proposed a pilot action to help the eight Member States with the highest levels of youth unemployment to re-allocate some of their EU structural funds allocations to tackle youth unemployment. The aim was to mobilize EU funding still available in the 2007–2013 programming period to support job opportunities for young people and to facilitate Small and Medium-Sized Enterprises' (SME) access to finance since SMEs constitute a major source of job creation across the EU. The pilot action focused on the eight Member States with levels of youth unemployment at rates over or around 30% at the end of 2011: Latvia, Greece, Ireland, Italy, Lithuania, Portugal, Slovakia and Spain. Action teams composed of national and Commission officials were set up and worked between February and May 2012 to target available funding. This pilot action has contributed to a significant mobilization of EU funds, including through further (re-) programming.

In February 2013, the European Council agreed to create the Youth Employment Initiative to increase the EU financial support available to the regions and individuals struggling most with youth employment and inactivity. In April 2013, the Youth Guarantee Recommendation was formally adopted to ensure young people's successful transition into work. All EU countries, including Latvia, have committed to the implementation of the Youth Guarantee in a Council Recommendation *of 22 April 2013 on establishing a Youth Guarantee*. The Youth Guarantee is a commitment by all Member States to ensure that all young people under the age of 25 years receive a good quality offer of employment, continued education, apprenticeship, traineeship within four months of becoming unemployed or leaving formal education. Youth unemployment in the EU has decreased from a peak of 24% in 2013 to 14% in 2019.

The country fiche for Latvia (May 2018) explains the detailed assessment of the Youth Guarantee implementation in the country.[38] Latvia presented a Youth Guarantee Implementation Plan on 20 December 2013, updated in April 2014. The scheme started in January 2014, targeting young people, not in employment, education or training aged 15–29 years. The Ministry of Welfare is in charge of establishing and managing the Youth Guarantee, while the State Employment Agency (SEA) and the State Education Development Agency (SEDA) are responsible for

37. http://ec.europa.eu/social/home.jsp, last visited 15 Dec. 2019.
38. https://ec.europa.eu/social/main.jsp?catId=1161&langId=en&intPageId=3341, last visited 15 Dec. 2019.

implementation. Other main actors involved are the Ministry of Science and Education and municipalities, and youth organizations. The Latvian Youth Guarantee is fully funded by the Youth Employment Initiative. As the EC published its Country Report on Latvia in 2018,[39] it shows several good trends regarding youth situation. Youth unemployment has declined as labour demand picked up. The employment rate of recent upper secondary VET graduates (74.8%) was similar to the EU average (75%), while, the proportion of students enrolled in VET programmes remains below the EU average (74.8%). In 2018, employment rate among young people (aged 15–24) constituted 33.1%, which is 0.1 percentage points higher than in 2017. The number of employed young people accounted for 57.4 thousand (59.1 thousand in 2017).

II. Data by Gender and Age Groups, Including Some Projections

20. The specific weight of women in the population of Latvia is very high (more than 50%; in 2018 in total 1,934,379 persons; 889,641 males; 1,044,738 females), which is among the highest in the world.[40] The Centre of Demography of the University of Latvia together with the CSB and Eurostat based on data from 2003 to 2004 made estimations for population projections of Latvia, which shows an increased proportion of men in 2030 – 46.4% (Tables 4 and 5).[41]

Table 4 Population Projections of Latvia (1,000 Persons)

	Year					
Producer of the Projections	*2000*	*2010*	*2020*	*2030*	*2040*	*2050*
University of Latvia Demography Centre, conditional real version, 1999	2,418[a]	2,275	2,170	2,115[d]		
Population Department of the UN Secretariat, medium version, 2001	2,421	2,288	2,161	2,015	1,874	1,744
US Population Census Bureau, main version, 2004	2,367[b]	2,252	2,142	2,019	1,887	1,755
Eurostat, CSB, University of Latvia Demography Centre, main version, 2004	2,319[c]	2,240	2,115	2,022	1,942	1,873

Notes: [a] 1998; [b] 2002; [c] 2004; [d] 2025.

39. https://ec.europa.eu/info/sites/info/files/2018-european-semester-country-report-latvia-en.pdf, last visited 15 Dec. 2019.
40. http://www.csb.gov.lv, last visited 31 Dec. 2019.
41. The Centre of Demography of the University of Latvia.

Table 5 Forecast for Number of Inhabitants and Gender – Age Composition for 2005–2035

All inhabitants							
Age	*2005*	*2010*	*2015*	*2020*	*2025*	*2030*	*2035*
0–14	341,776	306,492	327,444	341,753	334,295	305,054	273,510
15–24	359,504	326,278	235,494	191,139	207,993	230,070	239,380
25–49	816,469	802,804	795,285	770,589	705,599	656,525	608,263
50–59	276,010	296,744	306,201	286,773	275,816	276,939	287,228
60–64	130,221	117,945	125,152	136,789	136,867	123,846	129,226
65–74	229,413	222,818	201,094	200,738	220,850	234,424	225,603
75+	151,682	166,561	183,560	187,645	186,646	195,493	215,408
	2,305,075	2,239,642	2,174,230	2,115,426	2,068,066	2,022,351	1,978,618
Men							
0–14	174,715	157,117	167,405	174,813	171,352	156,887	140,914
15–24	183,320	166,268	120,271	97,920	106,040	117,064	121,957
25–49	401,007	396,089	394,323	382,166	349,583	324,726	301,539
50–59	123,986	134,450	140,032	132,585	129,469	130,876	135,477
60–64	54,106	49,179	52,587	58,495	59,352	54,815	58,278
65–74	85,397	82,535	74,850	75,925	85,379	92,833	91,563
75+	39,159	45,748	52,829	55,365	56,311	60,833	69,965
	1,061,690	1,031,386	1,002,297	977,269	957,486	938,034	919,693
Women							
0–14	167,061	149,375	160,039	166,940	162,943	148,167	132,596
15–24	176,184	160,010	115,223	93,219	101,953	113,006	117,423
25–49	415,462	406,715	400,962	388,423	356,016	331,799	306,724
50–59	152,024	162,294	166,169	154,188	146,347	146,063	151,751
60–64	76,115	68,766	72,565	78,294	77,515	69,031	70,948
65–74	144,016	140,283	126,244	124,813	135,471	141,591	134,040
75+	112,523	120,813	130,731	132,280	130,335	134,660	145,443
	1,243,385	1,208,256	1,171,933	1,138,157	1,110,580	1,084,317	1,058,925

Source: Pēteris Zvidriņš and Edvins Vitoliņš, 'Ielúkosimies nàkotnē: jaunàkàs demogràfiskàs prognozes. Demogràfiskà situàcija odien un rit. Stratēiskàs analizes komisija', *Zinâtniski pētnieciskie raksti* 3(4) 2005. Riga, Zinàtne, 2005, pp. 112–113.

21. Various researches[42] and prognoses show the gender–age composition of Latvia's population as 'far from harmonious' and very damaged. It has been influenced by wars, fluctuations of birth level, migration flows. Currently the demographic pyramid has a very narrow basis, which results from the declining birth rate after 1990. Among older people there are a high proportion of women, mainly because of the mortality rate in the group of working age men. In the near future, a small increase in the number of children is expected. However, after 2020 it will start to decline again in opposition to the old age group. The average age will increase relatively rapidly.

Following the post-enlargement opening of selected EU-15 labour markets, labour outflows from Latvia together with other Baltic countries and Poland intensified. Workers headed mainly to Ireland and the United Kingdom which, together with Sweden, opened labour markets for the EU-8 workers immediately after accession in 2004. These flows (also reflecting the legalization of already existing employment) may be temporary and primarily supporting local labour markets during economic upturns.[43]

Even though absorbed with a little adverse effect on the receiving countries, labour migration has had a substantial impact on the sending economies, pushing up wages and adding to skill shortages. Still, payments sent to Latvia by migrant workers went up to EUR 104 in 2008,[44] in 2016 up to 1,118 million (663 million intra-EU, 455 million extra-EU), in 2017 up to 1,124 million (650 million intra-EU, 466 million extra-EU), in 2018 up to 1,047 million (619 million intra-EU, 428 million extra-EU). Latvia's secondary income account (reflecting remittances from Latvians working abroad and including certain fiscal transfers from the EU) has remained positive since 2010. Latvia, Croatia and Bulgaria were most dependent on international remittances in the EU in 2018 (in Croatia 6.3% of GDP, Bulgaria and Latvia – both 3.6% of GDP.[45]

Relatively, the most significant outflow was observed in Latvia and other Baltic countries.[46] The leading destination country for Latvian citizens was the UK, followed by Ireland, Germany and recently also Norway. Large and growing Latvian and Lithuanian diaspora have emerged in Ireland, where they are among the top five groups of foreign nationals and the United Kingdom. During the economic crisis, migration has contributed to a decline in unemployment and real wage growth in general, as well as improvements in the labour market position of low skilled.

42. Including the Centre of Demography of the University of Latvia, the Central Statistical Bureau, the Eurostat, the Population Department of the UN Secretariat; Peteris Zvidriņš and Edvins Vitoliņš, 'Ielúkosimies nàkotnē: jaunàkàs demogràfiskàs prognozes. Demogràfiskà situàcija cdien un rit. Stratēiskàs analizes komisija', *Zinâtniski pētnieciskie raksti* 3(4) 2005, Riga, Zinàtne, 2005, pp. 112–113. https://osp.maps.arcgis.com/apps/MapSeries/index.html?appid=fa20eb678fe3495e89788d000bfec641, Women and Men in Baltic countries; last visited 15 Dec. 2019.
43. The World Bank EU 10 Regular Economic Report.
44. The Bank of Latvia, http://www.bank.lv, last visited 15 Dec. 2019.
45. https://ec.europa.eu/eurostat/statistics-explained/index.php/Special:Categories, last visited 15 Dec. 2019.
46. P. Kaczmarczyk and M. Okolski, 2008, 'Economic Impacts of Migration on Poland and the Baltic states', Fafo-paper 2008:01.

Through these channels and remittances migration thus helped to improve living standards. Overall, about two-thirds of Latvian migrant workers were sending money home between 2004 and 2009.[47]

Emigration has slowed after peaking during the recent economic crisis, but continues to exceed natural population decrease and has been higher than in any OECD country over the past decade.[48] According to CSB, in 2018, as a result of international long-term migration population of the country dropped by 4.9 thousand people, which is the lowest indicator recorded over the past twenty years, whereas the negative natural increase resulted in two times bigger reduction (of 9.5 thousand people).[49] From 2008 to 2016, the number of emigrants was prevailing over that of immigrants, while as emigration reduced the negative natural increase recorded in the past two years exceeded the negative migration flow difference. Over the last three years, the total population of the country has been reducing slower – the decline registered last year accounted for 0.74%, compared to 0.96% in 2016.

§4. Other Necessary Data, Including the Distinction Between the Private and Public Sectors

22. Regarding the structure of employment activities, instead of a single definition of the public or private sector, rather a functional approach is applied for identification. The public sector is composed of state and local government institutions and other organizations that are the subjects of public rights (public entities). Public entities are defined by the State Administration Structure Law[50] of the Republic of Latvia as being incipient legal persons of public rights, and derivative public entities that operate in accordance with principles of public rights. Derivative public entities are local government or other public entities that are established based on law or in accordance with the law. Derivative public entities have an autonomy that is set by law, including their budgets and property. The state administration led by the Cabinet of Ministers carries out administrative functions of the executive power (functions of state administration). The general government sector (S.13) in Latvia consists of three subsectors:

(i) central government sub-sector (S.1311);
(ii) local government sub-sector (S.1313);
(iii) social security fund sub-sector (S.1314).

Publicly derived persons include state founded universities, scientific institutes and their institutions.

47. The Post-Enlargement Migration Experience in the Baltic Labour Markets by Mihails Hazans, Kaia Philips, http://www.iza.org, last visited 3 Jun. 2016.
48. OECD Reviews of Labour Market and Social Policies: Latvia 2016, pp. 101–135.
49. https://www.csb.gov.lv/en/statistic, last visited 15 Dec. 2019.
50. http://www.mk.gov.lv/en/mk/darbibu-reglamentejosie-dokumenti/administration-structure-law/, last visited 31 Dec. 2019.

23. In 2018 there were 61,052 employees in the state budget financed establishments and enterprises, less than 11,000 of them are civil servants (in the private sector – 618,339; in the public sector – 290,685 persons)[51] In the ministries, and State Chancellery of Latvia are employed 7% of all persons employed in state budget financed institutions.[52] Since 2008 the number of persons employed in the state budget funded institutions has been reduced by 21% (from 77,295 persons in 2008).

24. As is the case with other small economies, the importance of SMEs to the domestic economy is higher than the EU average, even though the number of SMEs relative to Latvia's population is lower than in other EU countries. Most SMEs are represented in wholesale and retail trade and manufacturing, with a combined contribution of 44.9% to total SME value-added and 43.4% to SME employment. In Latvia SMEs account for 70% of value added and 79% of jobs, significantly higher than the respective EU averages of 56.8% and 66.4%. In 2013–2017, the value-added of Latvian SMEs rose by 25.6%. The major drivers of this growth are manufacturing, wholesale, retail trade, transportation and storage (Table 6).[53]

Table 6 Importance of SMEs

Class Size	*Number of Persons Employed*			*Value Added (Million EUR)*					
	Number	*%*	*EU-28*	*Number*	*%*	*EU-28*	*Value (Billion EUR)*	*%*	*EU-28*
Micro	104,795	92.1	93.1	208,970	33.4	29.4	2.5	20.9	20.7
Small	7,344	6.5	5.8	146,547	23.4	20.0	2.8	23.0	17.8
Medium	1,421	1.2	0.9	138,276	22.1	17.0	3.2	26.1	18.3
SMEs	113,560	99.8	99.8	493,793	79.0	66.4	8.5	70.0	56.8
Large	195	0.2	0.2	131,173	21.0	33.6	3.6	30.0	43.2
Total	113,755	100.0	100.0	624,966	100.0	100	12.1	100.0	100.0

Source: Eurostat SBS database, estimates for 2017.

§5. Underlying Social and Cultural Values of Society

25. Over the last twenty years, Latvia had managed to shift from a centrally planned socialist economy to a liberal market economy, in this process achieving a

51. http://data.csb.gov.lv, last visited 15 Dec. 2019.
52. Report of the Ministry of Finance, http://ww.fm.gov.lv, last visited 15 Dec. 2019.
53. SBA Fact sheet Latvia 2018, European Commission, Enterprise and Industry, http://www.ec.europa.eu, last visited 15 Dec. 2019.

relatively stable macroeconomic situation characterized by rapid growth rates though simultaneously featuring high inflation, low labour productivity as well as marked regional disparities. However, as of 2008 to 2011, the socio-economic situation witnessed considerable turbulence due to the evolving financial crisis of the country having a profound impact on the national economy as a whole.

26. Latvia's accession to the EU has presented both challenges and opportunities. It has provided many opportunities for the free movement of goods, services, and labour force. The availability of EU Structural Funds and the EU membership being a guarantee of investor confidence has triggered capital inflows. Investors' perception of Latvia as a location with capital yields has allowed an increase in productivity and contributed to income growth.

27. Latvian civic society is based on a common cultural space that is characterized by cultural diversity united by common values. Latvia's geopolitical situation and history have created a multicultural society in Latvia, which will become even more diverse due to globalization. Although Latvian society is shaped by a variety of cultures, there still is a lack of knowledge and understanding between different cultural groups, which stimulates collective prejudices, stereotypes and intolerance. In order to promote democracy and the development of civic society, as well to protect the rights of minorities, the government of Latvia had set as its objective to facilitate the formation of an integrated society founded on shared, fundamental mutual values.[54]

54. http://www.politika.lv, last visited 15 Dec. 2019.

Chapter 2. Definitions and Notions

§1. Distinction Between Labour Law (Industrial Relations) and Other Branches of Law, Especially Social Security Law

28. Social legislation in Latvia comprises labour law on the one hand and the social security law on the other. Latvian legislation provides for a compulsory social security system, which covers:

- maternity and sickness insurance;
- disability insurance;
- parental insurance;
- pension insurance;
- insurance against unemployment;
- insurance against accidents at work and occupational diseases;
- health insurance.

The social security system is administered by the State Social Insurance Agency (SSIA), which is a state institution under the supervision of the Ministry of Welfare, performing the public administration function in the area of social insurance and social services (administration of the social insurance state budget; registration of socially insured persons and their contributions into the socially insured person's personal accounts; providing social insurance and selected social assistance services to the population – pensions, benefits and allowances etc.).[55]

The state social security system guarantees a defined amount of compensation for loss of income in certain situations to persons paying social insurance contributions. The amount of compensation depends on the income from which the amount of the contribution has been calculated.

Social insurance contribution payments are calculated based on the likely risks for various groups of taxpayers.

From 1 January 2018 maximum amount of the object of the State social insurance mandatory contributions is EUR 55,000 per year. The object of mandatory contributions for a professional athlete is EUR 860 per year.

The object of mandatory contributions:

- for employees, with the exception of employees of micro-enterprises – all the income from employment, from which the individual income tax is withheld, without deducting the non-taxable minimum, tax incentives and deductible expenses;
- for professional sportsmen – EUR 860. If the salary of a professional sportsman is less, the employer of the sportsman is obliged to cover the difference in state social insurance contributions from his own funds;
- for self-employed persons – freely chosen income that is not less than the amount of the minimum monthly wage;

55. The State Social Insurance Agency, http://www.vsaa.gov.lv, last visited 15 Dec. 2019.

- for persons, who receive consideration for performing foster family's duties – EUR 171;
- for a person carrying out economic activity and paying a licence fee, the object of mandatory contribution is calculated by considering the appropriate mandatory contribution rate and the fact that 67% of the amount of license fee is the mandatory contributions made;
- for an employee of a micro-enterprise, the object of mandatory contribution is calculated according to the calculated amount of mandatory contributions (80% of the amount of micro-enterprise tax) in proportion to the number of employees in each month and the actual income of employees, applying the appropriate mandatory contribution rate;
- for employees paying the income tax of seasonal farm workers, the object of mandatory contribution is calculated in proportion to the payment to a special budget account, the employee's earned income, applying the appropriate mandatory contribution rate;
- for a person taking care of a child up to 1.5 years old and receiving the parents' benefit or allowance for childcare – EUR 171;
- for a person receiving the remuneration for the care of an adopted child – EUR 171;
- for a person receiving the childcare benefit for child with disability – EUR 71.14;
- for a person, who has been a resident of the particular country as the spouse of a soldier fulfilling official duties, except where the soldier is taking part in an international operation, military training, war games or is on mission – EUR 71.14;
- for a person, whose spouse fulfils the diplomatic and consular duties abroad and who is staying in the foreign country as the spouse of a person fulfilling the diplomatic and consular duties – EUR 71.14;
- for an unemployed person with disability – 50% of the previous year's average wage subject to insurance contributions;
- for an unemployed person with disability in connection with an accident at work or occupational disease – remuneration for the loss of ability to work;
- for a person receiving the unemployment benefit – the unemployment benefit;
- for a person receiving the sickness, maternity or paternity benefit – the sickness, maternity or paternity benefit;
- for a person engaged in paid temporary community work – EUR 71.14.

All employees who have reached 15 years of age employed by an employer – a domestic taxpayer, another Member State taxpayer or a branch of a merchant (permanent representation) of another Member State, persons taking care of a child who has not reached one and a half years of age and receiving allowance for childcare or parenting benefit, persons receiving unemployment benefit, persons with disability who are not registered as employees or mandatory socially insured as self-employed persons, persons receiving a childcare benefit for child with disability, persons receiving a maternity, paternity or sickness benefit, persons receiving an allowance for the care of an adopted child, persons receiving for performing foster family's duties, persons whose spouse (who has been granted a diplomatic rank in accordance with the Diplomatic and Consular Service Law) performs diplomatic and consular service in a foreign state and who stay in the relevant foreign state as a spouse of a person performing diplomatic and consular service, persons who are located in a relevant foreign state in the status of spouse of a soldier performing service duties, except in the cases where the soldier participates in an international operation, military training, manoeuvres or is on official travel, persons performing temporary paid social work, persons engaged in seasonal agricultural works and paying the income tax of seasonal farm workers, persons carrying out economic activity and paying a licence fee, and self-employed persons shall be subject to mandatory social insurance.

All domestic employees who have attained 15 years of age employed at a foreign employer and foreign employees at a foreign employer are subject to mandatory social insurance.

Persons who have reached 15 years of age, whose permanent place of residence is in the Republic of Latvia and who are not subject to mandatory social insurance in the Republic of Latvia, may join the state social insurance voluntarily in accordance with the procedures stipulated by the Cabinet of Ministers. A person who has not been granted a state old-age pension in accordance with the Law on State Pensions may join voluntarily the pension insurance and a spouse of a self-employed person who has not reached the age giving the right to receive the state old-age pension or whom the state old-age pension has not been granted (including before term) may join the pension insurance, disability insurance, maternity and sickness insurance, and parents' insurance voluntarily.

State compulsory social insurance contributions are made to the social insurance budget, entitling the contributor to general sickness, pension, maternity, and other benefits. The Law on State Social Insurance determines the application of mandatory tax payments to salaries received by employees (income gained by an employee from whom one deducts personal income tax and income of a self-employed person).[56] The rate of compulsory contributions, if an employee is insured against all types of social insurance, is 35.09% of which an employer pays 24.09%, and 11% is paid by an employee. Around 1% of the total rate of mandatory contributions is transferred for the financing of health care services. Health insurance is applicable to all employees and self-employed persons who have actually made mandatory contributions, incl. for health insurance, except employees of micro-enterprises (who are paying the micro-enterprise tax/for whom the micro-enterprise tax is paid), patent fee payers (who are paying the patent fee) and seasonal agricultural workers (who are paying the agricultural workers' income tax).

The members of the Latvian diaspora, who are not a subject to compulsory social security, can join the state pension insurance voluntarily.

29. According to the Law on State Social Insurance, the Cabinet of Ministers determines the mandatory contribution rate for persons subject to mandatory social insurance and the distribution thereof according to the types of social insurance for the following year.

---

56. http://www.vvc.gov.lv/export/sites/default/docs/LRTA/Likumi/On_State_Social_Insurance.doc, last visited 15 Dec. 2019.

An employee of a company paying the micro-enterprise tax may voluntarily join social insurance if the person is not an employee of another employer or is not mandatorily insured as a self-employed person. If an employee of a micro-enterprise is mandatorily insured for all types of social insurance, the person may voluntarily join all types of social insurance.

As of 1 January 2019, the solidarity tax rate is 25.50% from the amount which exceeds EUR 62,800 per year. The annual solidarity tax rate is calculated according to Article 18 of the Law on State Social insurance. Employer within the year calculates social tax rate as in standard case even when the income of employee exceeds EUR 62,800.

The same mandatory contribution rate, which is applied to a person's income up to the maximum amount of the object of mandatory contributions (EUR 62,800), must be applied to the object of the solidarity tax in the taxation year. Hence, if the employer calculated mandatory contributions by applying the rate of 35.09%, also the solidarity tax must be calculated by applying the same rate.

The difference between the actually paid solidarity tax, e.g., in the amount of 35.09%, and the calculated solidarity tax in the amount of 25.50%, is to be regarded as the solidarity tax overpayment and it shall be refunded.

In order to receive unemployment benefit in Latvia, persons must fulfil certain conditions, namely: they have to obtain the status of unemployed person at the SEA; their length of employment should be at least one year, and they must have paid mandatory social insurance contributions for no less than twelve months in the past sixteen months before obtaining the status of an unemployed person. The benefit is calculated in proportion to the total length of the insurance (employment) record and in accordance with the income from which unemployment contributions have been paid:

The length of the insurance (employment) record:	The amount of the benefit granted:
from 1 to 9 years (included)	50% of the average contributions' salary
from 10 to 19 years (included)	55% of the average contributions' salary
from 20 to 29 years (included)	60% of the average contributions' salary
30 years or more	65% of the average contributions' salary

30. The benefit is being paid to all unemployed for the duration of 8 months (starting from 1 January 2020), regardless of the length of their employment. Unemployed persons, who were granted this status up until 31 December 2019 – benefit pay-out duration is 9 months, and the benefit is paid out as follows:

- during the first three months – in the amount granted;
- during the next three months – 75% of the benefit granted;
- during the last three months – 50% of the benefit granted.

The benefit will be paid for the duration of eight months:

- during the first two months – in the amount granted;
- during the third and fourth month – 75% of the benefit granted;
- during the fifth and sixth month – 50% of the benefit granted;
- during the seventh and eighth month – 45% of the benefit granted.

31. The following support for families with children is provided in Latvia:

- *Maternity benefit* (to compensate the income not earned in the work while a woman is on the maternity leave, state grants a maternity benefit to each socially insured woman. The benefit is paid in two parts – for 56 or 70 days before childbirth and 56 or 70 days after childbirth. When allocating the maternity benefit, 56 and 56 calendar days (or 70 and 70 days) from maternity leave are summed up, resulting in 112 calendar days in total. The first part is paid for fifty-six or seventy days of the maternity leave. The benefit for seventy calendar days is paid to expectant mothers who are undergoing medical supervision from their twelfth week of pregnancy. The second part – for fifty-six or seventy calendar days – is paid after childbirth. The benefit for seventy days can be obtained, if: (a) the mother has had health problems during her pregnancy, childbirth, or postpartum period; (b) Two or more babies are born. The maximum period for which the maternity benefit can be obtained is 140 days. It is added to the maternity leave. Therefore, the state can allocate maternity benefit for seventy calendar days. A woman can receive an additional fourteen-day leave also in case of health problems during the pregnancy, delivery, or post-delivery period or if two or more children are delivered. Also, in this case, a fourteen-day additional leave is added to the maternity leave and benefit is paid for seventy calendar days in total. The benefit shall be granted in the amount of 80% of the average insurance contributions salary of the applicant. The average insurance contributions salary of an employee is calculated for a period of twelve calendar months ending two months before the month in which the pregnancy leave began. For self-employed women, the average insurance contributions salary shall be calculated in accordance with the average contributions made during the period of the last twelve months ending three months before the quarter in which the pregnancy leave began. The benefit must be requested within six months from the first day of the maternity leave. From 1 January 2020, women who have lost their status as an employed or self-employed worker not earlier than sixty days before maternity leave shall also be entitled to maternity allowance. From 1 September 2020, persons who are or have been required to make compulsory contributions to maternity insurance in the Republic of Latvia are entitled to maternity benefit not less than three months during the six months preceding the month in which the insured event occurred (first day of the maternity leave), or not less than six months in the last twenty-four months. For covered events occurring 1 September 2020, or later, in determining entitlement to maternity benefit, the eligibility period conditions determine whether the person's compulsory contributions have been made within a specified period.[57]

- *Childbirth benefit* (to support the families with the newborn the state grants a lump sum as childbirth benefit, which is granted to one of the child's parents or to the person who has guardianship over a child up to the one year of age. The amount of childbirth benefit is EUR 421.17 per each newborn).[58]
- *Paternity benefit* (fathers of a newborn can use ten days paternity leave until the infant is two months old. Socially insured fathers also could receive the paternity benefit. The benefit shall be granted in the amount of 80% of the average insurance contributions salary of the applicant. The average insurance contributions salary of an employee for receiving of the paternity benefit is calculated for twelve calendar months ending two months prior to the month in which the leave concerning the child's birth has begun. For a self-employed person, the average insurance contributions salary shall be calculated for twelve months ending one quarter before the quarter in which the leave in relation to the child's birth begins. Paternity benefit is granted to one of the parents upon adoption of a child aged up to three years who is in out-of-family care. Parents who have adopted a child up to the age of 18 years have the right to receive a paternity benefit if the court judgment regarding adoption has entered into effect after 1 September 2019 and the employer has granted a leave of ten calendar days in relation to the adoption of a child).
- *Family state benefit:* the benefit for the first child in the family is EUR 11.38 a month. The benefit for the second child is EUR 22.76 (twice the amount), for the third child – EUR 34.14 (three times the amount for the first child), for the fourth and any next child – EUR 50.07. The benefit is granted to one of the child's parents, custodian or person who is actually bringing up a child and approved by orphan's court decision. The benefit is granted for each child raised in the family from when the child becomes one year old until the age of 15. If the child after reaching the age of 15 years continues to study in a general or vocational education institution (even if he/she receives scholarship), then the benefit is paid until the age of 20 years (if he or she has not entered into marriage). When the amount of the state family benefit is set, all of the children of the applicant are taken into account in the total number of children in the applicant's family – including the children for which the benefit is not paid anymore because the child has reached the age of 20 years or if he/she after getting 15 years old does not study, as well as deceased children of the applicant.[59]

57. http://www.likumi.lv, last visited 31 Dec. 2019.
58. http://www.likumi.lv – Regulation of the Cabinet of Ministers No. 1546 'Regulation Regarding the Procedures for Granting and Payment of the Child Birth Benefit' and http://www.vvc.gov.lv/export/sites/default/docs/LRTA/Likumi/Law_on_State_Social_Allowances_.doc, last visited 15 Dec. 2019.
59. http://www.vvc.gov.lv/export/sites/default/docs/LRTA/Likumi/Law_on_State_Social_Allowances_.doc, last visited 15 Dec. 2019.

- *Supplement to the family state benefit*: additional payment to the state family benefit for raising two and more children aged from 1 year to 20 years. For two children – EUR 10 per month; for three children – EUR 66 per month; for each of the following children – EUR 50 more than for the previous child, namely: for four children – EUR 116 per month; for five children – EUR 166 per month; for six children – EUR 216 per month, etc. For the calculation of the amount of the additional payment, the number of children is specified differently from the number determined in case of the state family benefit. The amount of the additional payment does not take into account, and the number of children does not include the children for whom the state family benefit is not granted and paid, for example, deceased children; children regarding whom the benefit is received by the other parent or another beneficiary; children who are more than 20 years old; children who have not reached the age of 20 years yet, but who after reaching the age of 15 years do not study; children who have not reached the age of one year and for whom the state family benefit is not granted; and other cases when the state family benefit for a child of the applicant is not granted and paid. If the payment of the state family is stopped for a child (e.g., the child does not study after reaching the age of 15 years), the amount of the additional payment is recalculated, or the payment is stopped. The application for granting of the family state benefit and the supplement must be submitted not later than within six months from the moment when the right is created. If the benefit is applied for later, it is granted only for the previous 6 months before the application for the benefit.
- *Child care benefit for child with disability*[60] (to provide additional support to families with a child who has severe functional disorders; the benefit is allocated to the person who is taking care of child with disability in the age up to 18 years or up to the period when the established disability or statement on necessity for a special care is terminated. A person can receive benefit also in case if he/she is employed. From July 1, 2019, the amount of child care benefit for a child with disability is EUR 313.43 per month (until 30 June 2019, it was EUR 231.43 per month). In order to receive childcare benefit for a child with disability, a child must have a disability established by the State Medical Commission for the Assessment of Health Condition and Working Ability, and the Opinion issued stating the need for special care. Information about the child with disability for whom the opinion on the necessity for special care concerning functional severe disorders has been issued will be submitted to the SSIA by the State Medical Commission for Expert-Examinations of Health and Working Ability in electronic form.
- The state also grants an *additional payment to family state benefit for a child with disability* – EUR 106.72 per month. Supplement to the family state benefit for a child with disability is granted from the day of establishment of the status of a child with disability until the day when the child with disability reaches the age of 18 years, regardless of the payment of the family state benefit. Information about a child with disability is submitted to the SSIA by the State Medical Commission for Expert-Examinations of Health and Working Ability in electronic form. The application for granting of the supplement to the family state benefit

60. https://likumi.lv/doc.php?id=202852&from=off, last visited 31 Dec. 2019.

must be submitted not later than within six months from the moment when the right is created. If the benefit is applied for later, it is granted only for the previous six months before the application for the benefit;

- *State support to the children who have the celiac disease* without formally stated disability (to help those parents whose children are suffering from celiac disease, the state provides additional support to these families for the purchase of gluten-free food items). The amount of the support corresponds to the amount of the additional payment to the state family allowance for a child with disability, EUR 106.71 per month. The support is provided for children up to 18 years of age (have not come of age) and children after reaching 18 years of age (after coming of age), if the child is studying at an institution of general education or vocational education and has not reached 20 years of age or is a day student at an institution of higher education (full-time studies) and is no older than 24 years of age. The support is granted for a period until the repeated examination set in the health certificate (but no longer than two years). The support is provided to one of the parents of the child; an adopter; a guardian or a member of the foster family; the person taking care of the child before the adoption; another person actually taking care of the child, if a corresponding decision of the orphan's court has been made for the protection of the child's interests; to the child after he/she has come of age; to the child after he/she becomes 15 years old, if a corresponding decision of the orphan's court has been made for the protection of the child's interests;
- *Allowance to compensate transport expenses of persons with mobility disabilities*[61] is granted to a person to whom or to whose child a disablement has been specified and to whom an opinion of the State Medical Commission for the Assessment of Health Condition and Working Ability regarding the determination of medical indications for the purchase of a specially fitted car and the receipt of an allowance has been issued. If the allowance is requested for a child with disability, it is granted for one of the parents, guardian or person who actually raises the child, including a foster family if the child has been given for family for a period that does not exceed a period of six months. The amount of the allowance is EUR 79.68 for each six months period. The allowance is paid twice a year for every completed six months counting from the day when the opinion of the State Medical Commission for Expert-Examinations of Health and Working Ability was issued until the moment when the term of the established disability ends. The application must be submitted not later than within 6 months from the moment when the right is created. If the benefit is applied for later, it is granted only for the previous six months before the application for the benefit;
- *Parents' benefit* (the parental benefit is granted to one of the parents if a parent is caring for a child younger than one-year-old and a parent is employed on the day the benefit is approved (as an employee or self-employed person). The average monthly insurance contribution wage is calculated for a period of twelve months, which has ended two months before the month from which the benefit is granted. For a self-employed person, the average wage subject to insurance contributions per calendar day shall be calculated according to the actual contribution made in

61. https://likumi.lv/doc.php?id=202851&from=off, last visited 31 Dec. 2019.

the last twelve-month period that ends a quarter (three months) prior to the quarter, on which the parents' benefit has been granted. There is an option to choose the duration of receiving the benefit, and the amount of the benefit is established according to the chosen duration of receiving the benefit: (a) until the child reaches the age of 1 – to the amount of 60% of the recipient's average wage subject to insurance contributions or (b) until the child reaches the age of 1.5 – to the amount of 43.75% of the recipient's average wage subject to insurance contributions. If the choice is made regarding the duration of receiving the benefit (until the child reaches the age of 1 or 1.5) and the benefit is granted, the chosen duration in case of the same child may not be changed. The recipient of the parents' benefit, who resumes work, discontinuing the parental leave, or resumes earning income as a self-employed, the benefit is paid to the amount of 30% of the benefit granted. Also for a person who, on the day of requesting the benefit, is not on the parental leave or earns income as a self-employed person the benefit is calculated in the amount of 30% of the benefit granted (depending on what duration of receiving the benefit has been chosen by the recipient – until the child reaches the age of 1, in the amount of 60% of the average wage; or until the child reaches the age of 1.5, in the amount of 43.75% of the average wage). For example, the parents' benefit is granted for the period until the child reaches the age of 1, in the amount of 60% of the recipient's average wage subject to insurance contributions – EUR 15 per calendar day. After discontinuation of parental leave and resuming work, the benefit will be recalculated to the amount of 30% of EUR 15 = EUR 4.50 per calendar day. A person is entitled to simultaneously receive the parents' benefit (until the child reaches the age of 1 or 1.5, depending on the option selected) and the allowance for child care, the amount of which is EUR 171 a month until the child reaches the age of 1.5. From 1 January 2020 women who are not employed on the day of granting the benefit (are not regarded as an employees or self-employed in accordance with the law 'On State Social Insurance'), yet who have been granted maternity benefit in the following cases: as a woman who has lost the status of employee or self-employed person no more than sixty days before the date when maternity leave starts, as a woman who has lost the status of employee due to company liquidation 210 days before the date when maternity leave starts, or has lost the status of employee or self-employed person during maternity leave (while maternity benefit is received) are also entitled to parents' benefit. That means if maternity benefit has been granted to a woman, she is also entitled to receive parents' benefit for this child. From 1 September 2020 persons, for which compulsory contributions for parents' insurance have been made or had to be made in the Republic of Latvia:

for at least 3 months in the period of the last 6 months before the month when the insurance event has occurred, or for at least 6 months in the last twenty-four months are also entitled to parents' benefit. For insurance events occurring on 1 September 2020 or later, when determining rights to benefit, conformity to the qualification period conditions shall be ascertained primarily, i.e., it shall be determined whether compulsory contributions for the specified time period have been made for the person. In addition to the basic sum of the child allowance, for every next child, an extra bonus is assigned for the care of twins or several children born at a single delivery. If twins were born, then the person, who is taking care of the twins or several children born at a single birth, will receive bonus, besides the child allowance: up until the child is 1.5 years old – EUR 171 per month for each next child, and aged between 1.5 and 2 years – EUR 42.69 per month for each next child. The application must be submitted not later than within six months from the moment when the right is created. If the benefit is applied for later, it is granted only for the previous six months before the application for the benefit.

- *Allowance for childcare* (allowance to a person taking care of a child that has not reached the age of 2 – to one of the child's parents or the guardian or another person actually taking care of and raising the child according to the decision of the orphan's court. In case the parent is not a socially insured person, the allowance for child care is granted as of the day of the birth of the child, provided that no maternity benefit, parents' benefit or allowance for childcare is granted to the other parent for the same period of time in connection with the birth and taking care of the same child. If a parent is socially insured (employee or self-employed), he/she is granted parent benefit and child allowance for taking care of one and the same child. Both benefits can be received at the same time if a maternity benefit has not been granted for the same child for the same period. It should be noted that the benefits before are granted to one person for taking care of a child for a specific period. Therefore, the parents have to agree on who will receive both the parents' benefit and allowance for child care, as both benefits for taking care of a child are granted to one of the parents (one person). The rates of the benefits for a person taking care of a child that has not reached the age of 1.5 – EUR 171 a month; for a person taking care of a 1.5–2 years old child – EUR 42.69 a month. If twins or triplets have been born in the family, a premium is added to the basic amount of the allowance for child care for each next child: for a person taking care of twins or more children born in the same labour that have not reached the age of 1.5 – EUR 171 a month for each next child; for a person taking care of twins or more children born in the same labour and aged 1.5–2 – EUR 42.69 a month for each next child. Application for granting of the allowance for child care must be submitted no later than within six months from the moment of acquiring the right. If the application is submitted later, the allowance will be granted only for the six previous months before the day of requesting the allowance.[62]
- *Sickness benefit* (for sick child care under the age of 14 is granted and paid for the period of incapacity for work from the first to the fourteenth day and from the fifteenth to the twenty-first day – in the cases when the child receives health care at the hospital. From 1 January 2020 for children diagnosed with severe illnesses, sickness benefit shall be granted for the care of a child up to the child reaching the age of 18. These are cases when doctors' council of the state limited liability company 'Bērnu klīniskās universitātes slimnīca' has issued an opinion (opinion of doctors' council), stating that constant presence of a parent is necessary due to severe illness, as a result of which the child requires long-term treatment at an

62. http://likumi.lv/doc.php?id=202854, last visited 31 Dec. 2019.

in-patient medical treatment institution; child care benefit for a child with disability has been granted for the child. SSIA receives the opinion of doctors' council electronically, and parents do not have to submit this document when requesting sickness benefit. SSIA also holds information about children with granted child care benefit for a child with disability. In case of illness of a child aged up to 18 years with diagnosed severe illness, and if the doctor's council has issued an opinion on necessity of constant presence of a parent in addition to sick-leave certificate B, SSIA shall grant and pay sickness benefit for a time period: in case of continuous illness of a child – for the time prescribed by the doctors' council, which cannot exceed three months at a time. In total no more than twenty-six weeks (half-year), counting from the first day of illness of the child. If a child is ill with breaks – no more than for three years in a period of five years. The doctors' council may provide for the necessity of the constant presence of a parent no more than for three months at a time. In cases when treatment takes a very long time, and the child requires the presence of a parent, two opinions may be issued for one continuous case of illness. If an opinion of the doctors' council is not issued, then rights to receive sickness benefit for care of an ill child are determined in accordance with general procedure. Namely, the same as in cases when a child aged up to 14 years are taken care of. In case of illness of a child aged up to 18 years for which child care benefit for a child with disability has been granted, sickness benefit is granted and paid as follows: in case of continuous illness of a child – no longer than twenty-six weeks (half-year), counting from the first day of illness of the child; if a child is ill with breaks – no more than for three years in a period of five years. Therefore, if the necessity for special care has been determined for a child by the State Medical Commission of Health and Capacity to Work, based on which child care benefit for a child with disability has been granted, an opinion of doctors' council is not required for granting sickness benefit. In both cases, the conditions for payment of sickness benefit are applicable regardless of whether the child is taken care of by one parent (person) for the entire time of illness, or by several people by turns, as well as regardless of the cause of illness. For the first ten days of the sickness, the employer shall pay sick pay to the following amount: (a) for the second and third day of the sickness – not less than 75% of average earnings of beneficiary; (b) from the fourth to the tenth day of the sickness – not less than 80% of average earnings of the beneficiary. From the eleventh day of sickness, the State Social Insurance Agency shall grant a sickness benefit in the amount of 80% of the average contributions' salary of the beneficiary. The average contributions salary of an employee is calculated under the payments made during the last twelve months, ending one quarter (three months) before the quarter, in which the incapacity for work began. The benefit must be requested within six months from the first day of the temporary disability.

– *Foster family allowance*[63] (the entitlement to receive an allowance for the fulfilment of foster family duties for a family or person who has acquired the status of

63. http://www.likumi.lv, Regulation of the Cabinet of Ministers No. 1549 of 22 Dec. 2009 Procedures for the Granting and Disbursement of the Remuneration for the Fulfilment of Foster Family Duties, last visited 15 Dec. 2019.

a foster family and who according to a decision by an orphan's court and an agreement between a municipality and a foster family has been fostered a child for at least one month). Consideration is not granted to foster families who have acquired the status of a specialized foster family. The amount of consideration for performing custodian's duties depends on the number of foster children in the foster family: per one child placed in the foster family – EUR 171 per month; per two children placed in the foster family – EUR 222.30 per month; per three and more children – EUR 273.60 per month. If the number of children in the foster family changes, the amount of consideration is recalculated. If the number of children in the foster family increases, the amount of consideration is adjusted from the day when the child is placed in the foster family. In turn, if the number of foster children decreases, the amount of consideration is adjusted from the first day of the month following the month when the orphan's court takes a decision on the termination of the placement of the child in the foster family. From 1 January 2018 for foster parents, who receive consideration for performing custodian's duties and who are not socially insured persons (for instance, they are not employed or self-employed), social insurance contributions are made for pension insurance, disability insurance and unemployment insurance. Documents for the granting of the allowance shall be submitted within six months after a child was fostered according to a decision by an orphan's court and an agreement between a municipality and a foster family.

– *The benefit to a custodian for supporting a child* (the guardian's allowance for a dependent child). The amount of the benefit is: from the birth of the child till he/she reaches the age of 7 years – EUR 107.5; from the child's age of 7 years till the age of 18 years – EUR 129.[64] The allowance is granted for children under guardianship, who have been assigned a personal identification number, except when a child has been issued a temporary residence permit. If the child receives a survivor's pension, the state social security benefit due to the loss of a breadwinner, means of subsistence from the Administration of the Maintenance Guarantee Fund or the state family benefit, then the allowance for the dependent child will be reduced by the amount of the survivor's pension, the state social security benefit, means of subsistence and the state family benefit. If the insurance indemnity after the loss of a supporter is granted regarding the child, the benefit for supporting a child is reduced by the amount of the indemnity. Application for granting the benefit must be submitted no later than six months from the occurrence of such rights. When applying for the benefit later, it shall be granted only for the six months before the date of the application.
– *Consideration for performing custodian's duties* (an allowance for the fulfilment of a guardian's duties to the guardian for children in his/her guardianship. Consideration is granted to a member of the foster family (a person), which has acquired the status of a foster family and which according to the resolution of the orphan's court and the agreement between the municipality and the foster family has been fostered a child for at least one month. Consideration is not granted to

64. http://www.likumi.lv, Regulation of the Cabinet of Ministers No. 1643 of 22 Dec. 2009 Procedures for the Granting and Disbursement of Guardian's Allowance for a Dependent Child, last visited 15 Dec. 2019.

foster families who have acquired the status of a specialized foster family. From 1 January 2018, the amount of consideration for performing custodian's duties depends on the number of foster children in the foster family: per one child placed in the foster family – EUR 171 per month; per two children placed in the foster family – EUR 222.30 per month; per three and more children – EUR 273.60 per month. If the number of children in the foster family changes, the amount of consideration is recalculated. If the number of children in the foster family increases, the amount of consideration is adjusted from the day when the child is placed in the foster family. In turn, if the number of foster children decreases, the amount of consideration is adjusted from the first day of the month following the month when the orphan's court takes a decision on the termination of the placement of the child in the foster family.

– *Consideration for the care of an adopted child* (Consideration and additional payment are granted to the adopter who, according to the resolutions of the orphan's court before the approval of the adoption by the court, has taken into care and supervision the child to be adopted. Consideration and parents' benefit cannot be received at the same time for the same child. The adopter, who is taking care of a child under the age of 1.5 years and who is on vacation related to the child care, can choose either to receive consideration, or the parents' benefit. If before the adoption according to the resolution of the orphan's court several children are placed into care, an additional payment in amount of EUR 171 per month is granted for every following child simultaneously put into care. The documents for granting of the remuneration must be submitted within 6 months after the day, when the adopter starts taking care of the child according to the decision of the orphan's court. The amount of consideration depends on the age of the child to be adopted and the fact of employment of the adopter (is he/she is employed or self-employed, or not), as well as on the fact of being on unpaid vacation due to the need to take care of the child.

Adopter's Employment	*Age of the Child to Be Adopted*	*Amount of Consideration per Month*
Not employed	From 0 till 18 years	EUR 171
Employed (being on leave related to child care does not influence the amount of consideration)	From 8 till 18 years	

Adopter's Employment	*Age of the Child to Be Adopted*	*Amount of Consideration per Month*
Employed and not on leave related to the child care	From 0 till 7 years, incl.	EUR 171 If he/she decides to receive the parents' benefit, consideration is not granted
Employed and on leave related to the child care		EUR 535.09 (if the allowance was granted in 2019) EUR 489.05 if the allowance was granted in 2018)
Employed part time, up to 20 hours per week		70% of the average insurance contributions salary (in the calendar year ending the year before the year when consideration is granted) If he/she decides to receive the parents' benefit, consideration is not granted

- *Remuneration for the care of an adopted child*[65] (The remuneration is granted to the adopter after the court judgment on approval of the adoption comes into force. Remuneration for the adoption of a child is paid for each child, who has been in out-of-family care (in an institution of out-of-family care, a foster family, living with a guardian). The remuneration is not granted if a person has adopted a child of his/her spouse. The amount of remuneration for the adoption of a child is EUR 1,422.87. The documents for granting of the remuneration must be submitted within six months after the day when the adoption is approved.
- *Child adoption benefit* (from 1 July 2019, adopters have rights to a new state social benefit – child adoption benefit). The adopters whose permanent residence is in Latvia, who have been allocated a personal identity number and whose adopted children have been allocated a personal identity number have rights to receive the benefit. The amount of the benefit per month: from the child's birth until reaching the age of 7 years – EUR 107.50; from the moment of reaching the age of 7 years until reaching the age of 18 years – EUR 129. The benefit is granted for each adopted child to one of the child's parents who has adopted and is raising a child who has been in out-of-family care prior to the adoption (in an institution, in guardianship, in a foster family) and whose adopted children have

65. Law on State Social Allowances and Cabinet Regulation No. 1533 of 22 Dec. 2009 'Procedures for the Granting and Disbursement of Remuneration for Adoption of a Child', www.likumi.lv, last visited 31 Dec. 2019.

not reached the age of 18 years as at 1 July 2019, regardless of when the court ruling on approval of the adoption has become effective. The benefit is not granted if the other spouse's child is adopted. An application to grant the benefit must be submitted within six months from the moment the rights arise. If the benefit is claimed later, it will be granted only for the previous six months, counting from the day of claiming the benefit. Child adoption benefit is paid at the same time as other benefits that are granted to the adopter for raising and taking care of a child.

32. Labour law in Latvia regulates the civil law relationship which emerges if an employee performs work for an employer.[66] Unlike to businessman and craftsman (self-employment), an employee works under subordination of employer. Article 3 of the Latvian Labour Law[67] states that an employee is a natural person who, on the basis of an employment contract for agreed work remuneration, performs specific work under the guidance of an employer. The labour law does not apply to a self-employed worker or a performer of a particular job under the civil law provisions (independent contractor or service provider).

33. The Civil law provides that if the aim is not working itself, but rather a specific result of work, such as completion of a particular product or project, the contract should not be regarded as an employment contract but rather as service contract (Civil Law, Article 2179).[68] Under a service contract, one of the parties (contractor) undertakes to provide for the other party (customer) a specific piece of work, to produce a defined product or to implement a particular project for which agreed remuneration should be paid. According to the service contract, contractors must perform the work with their tools and equipment, meaning that they are responsible for arranging the place of work. The service contract thus differs from the employment contract in that it does not include clauses on working time and job responsibilities and does not require the employer to assume obligations towards the worker. The customer (employer) has no obligation to pay for vacation time or the national public holidays. As part of an employment contract, the employee receives a monthly salary, whereas, in the case of a service contract, the worker receives remuneration for the completed work.

Some experts[69] have previously noted the potential disadvantages of service contracts in respect of fewer guarantees for workers. As service contracts offer certain advantages to the employer, their use is becoming more common. Thus, employers are more likely to conclude a service contract when they require a specific project

66. Kaspars Balodis, 'Levads civiltiesibàs', *Zvaigzne ABC*, 2007, Riga, p. 41.
67. http://www.vvc.gov.lv/export/sites/default/docs/LRTA/Likumi/Labour_Law.doc, last visited 15 Dec. 2019.
68. http://www.vvc.gov.lv/export/sites/default/docs/LRTA/Likumi/The_Civil_Law.doc, last visited 15 Dec. 2019.
69. Mihails Hazans, Trends in conditions of work and employment in Latvia, report prepared in the framework of ILO-EC Project Working and employment condition in new member states: interaction and socio-economic impact.

to be done. Occasionally, such workers may be hired as a substitute for employees or as a possible selection mechanism for future recruitment on a permanent employment contract.

When a self-employed worker is, in fact, working in a relationship subordinate to his employer, such worker may be recognized as an employee by the State Revenue Service and the State Labour Inspectorate (SLI), thus triggering tax/fines consequences for failure to comply with tax and employment legislation and the employer may be ordered to enter into the employment contract with respective worker.

§2. Definitions of Labour Law and Its Concepts

34. Self-employed persons in Law on Social Insurance are individuals who are not employees (employment contract) and who earn income (or revenue) by doing individual work.[70] These include recipients of royalties, sworn notaries, sworn auditors, sworn solicitors; physicians, pharmacists, veterinaries, optometrists in individual practice; owners of farms or fishing undertaking, who not being in legal employment relationship with an administrative authority of his or her farm (fishing undertaking), performs the management function of such a farm (fishing undertaking) if, under the procedures laid down in law, a manager (director) has not been appointed (elected) in such a farm (fishing undertaking); sworn bailiffs, sole traders (merchants), individual merchant who is driving a taxi vehicle for commercial carriage of passengers and others who have registered as payers of taxes on income earned through economic activity.

35. An employer in the meaning of labour law is a natural or legal person or a partnership with legal capacity that, based on an employment contract, employs at least one employee.[71] Social security legislation[72] in the Law on State Social Insurance defines an employer as 'a legal or natural person, partnership with legal capacity, a taxpayer of other European Union Member State, Swiss Confederation or European Economic Area Member State or a branch of a merchant (permanent representation) of other Member State or a lessee of personnel who uses the services of such micro-enterprise that provides labour force ensuring services within the meaning of section 17.2 of the law On Personal Income Tax,[73] as well as a domestic taxpayer – a lessee of personnel leased by a foreign taxpayer who employs an employee or pays for the work of an employee'.

36. An employee in social insurance legislation[74] is defined as:

70. http://www.likumi.lv, Law on Social Insurance, last visited 31 Dec. 2019.
71. Article 4, Labour Law, http://www.vvc.gov.lv/export/sites/default/docs/LRTA/Likumi/Labour_Law.doc, last visited 31 Dec. 2019.
72. Article 1, Law on State Social Insurance, http://www.vvc.gov.lv/export/sites/default/docs/LRTA/Likumi/On_State_Social_Insurance.doc; last visited 31 Dec. 2019.
73. www.likumi.lv, last visited 31 Dec. 2019.
74. Article 1, Law on State Social Insurance, http://www.vvc.gov.lv/export/sites/default/docs/LRTA/Likumi/On_State_Social_Insurance.doc, last visited 31 Dec. 2019.

(a) a person who, on the basis of a contract of employment for an agreed work remuneration, performs specific work under the management of an employer, excluding micro-enterprise employee;[75]
(b) a member of the *Saeima*, a local government councillor, a member of the Cabinet of Ministers, a member of the board of directors, council of a commercial company, head clerk, controller, volunteer probation officer of the State Probation Service, as well as another person holding a position which gives the right to remuneration, if remuneration has been set in fact;
(c) a person who has entered into a work-performance contract, a sharecropping contract or a carriage contract provided for in Part IV, Chapter 15 of the Civil Law and has not registered as an economic activity income taxpayer;
(d) an official of an institution of the Ministry of the Interior system and Prisons Administration with a special service rank, an official of a State security institution or a military person of a unit subordinate to the Ministry of Defence;
(e) a state civil servant;
(f) an authorised representative of a foreign merchant, who not being in employment legal relationships with such merchant, represents those activities, which are related to the branches of the foreign merchant,
(g) micro-enterprise employee;
(h) a person who is employed in the Republic of Latvia by a foreign taxpayer having a permanent representation in the Republic of Latvia as well as a person who is leased to a domestic taxpayer by a foreign taxpayer – a lessee of personnel;
(i) a person who has concluded a service (work performance), sharecropping or carriage contract, as specified in Chapter 15, Part IV of the Civil Law of Latvia, and in respect of whom at least one of the features listed in Article 8(2.2) of the Law on Personal Income Tax is determined;
(j) an employee of micro-enterprise that provides labour force ensuring services within the meaning of section 17.2 of the Law on Personal Income Tax;[76]
(k) a convicted person who is employed while serving the sentence of deprivation of liberty;
(l) a board member of a capital company if the turnover of the capital company in the current month of the taxation year exceeds the minimum monthly wage stipulated by the Cabinet of Ministers multiplied by the coefficient 5 and in the relevant month the capital company does not have any employees or the object of mandatory contributions of all employees is less than the monthly wage stipulated by the Cabinet of Ministers;
(m) a person who within the meaning of the law On Personal Income Tax is employed in seasonal agricultural work and pays the seasonal agricultural worker income tax;
(n) a person who after the termination of the legal employment relationship has an agreement regarding the restriction of the occupational activity of the employee (restriction on competition);

75. Micro-enterprise Tax Law, http://www.vvc.gov.lv/advantagecms/LV/meklet/meklet_dokumentus.html?query=micro&resultsPerPage=10, last visited 31 Dec. 2019.
76. http://www.likumi.lv, last visited 31 Dec. 2019.

(o) a person who is driving a vehicle in the commercial carriage of passengers by a taxi, except for an individual merchant;
(p) a person to whom State aid for the payment of taxes are applied in accordance with the Law on Aid for the Activities of Start-up Companies;
(q) a professional athlete;
(r) an owner of a farm (fishing undertaking) who is in the legal employment relationship with his or her farm (fishing undertaking).

37. A self-employed person[77] is a person who earns income (or revenue) as:

(a) a person who performs individual work;
(b) a person whose permanent place of residence is in the Republic of Latvia and who receives a royalty (copyright or neighbouring rights remuneration), except for an heir to copyright and a successor in interest to other copyright;
(c) a sworn notary;
(d) a sworn advocate;
(e) a sworn auditor;
(f) a doctor in practice, a pharmacist in practice, a veterinary practitioner, an optometrist in practice;
(g) another natural person whose permanent place of residence is in the Republic of Latvia and who has registered as an economic activity income tax payer;
(h) an owner (owners) of a farm (fishing undertaking) who, not being in employment legal relations with an administrative authority of his or her farm (fishing undertaking), performs the management function of such a farm (fishing undertaking) if, in accordance with the procedures prescribed by law, a manager (director) has not been appointed (elected) in such a farm (fishing undertaking);
(i) a person whose permanent place of residence is in the Republic of Latvia and whose work is remunerated from foreign technical assistance resources and loans from international financial institutions granted to the Republic of Latvia;
(j) a sworn bailiff; and
(k) an individual merchant, including an individual merchant who is driving a taxi vehicle for commercial carriage of passengers.

38. The Commercial Law[78] provides a definition of 'undertaking' in Article 1840: 'An undertaking is an organizational, economical unit. The undertaking includes both tangible and intangible things belonging to a merchant, as well as other economic benefits (value), which are utilized by the merchant to perform commercial activities.' Within the meaning of the Labour Law,[79] an undertaking means 'any organizational unit in which an employer employs his or her employees'.

77. Article 1, Law on Social Security,, last visited 31 Dec. 2019.
78. http://www.vvc.gov.lv/export/sites/default/docs/LRTA/Likumi/The_Commercial_Law.doc, last visited 31 Dec. 2019.
79. Article 5, Labour Law, http://www.vvc.gov.lv/export/sites/default/docs/LRTA/Likumi/Labour_Law.doc, last visited 31 Dec. 2019.

39. According to the State Civil Service Law[80] a civil servant is a person who in a direct administration institution forms the policy or development strategy of a sector, coordinates the activity of a sector, distributes or controls financial resources, formulates regulatory enactments or controls the observance thereof, prepares or issues administrative documents, and prepares or takes other decisions related to the rights of individuals. A civil servant in the specialized state civil service is a person who performs the functions of civil servant, i.e. forms the policy or development strategy of a sector, coordinates the activity of a sector, distributes or controls financial resources, formulates regulatory enactments or controls the observance thereof, prepares or issues administrative documents, and prepares or takes any other decisions related to the rights of individuals in the diplomatic and consular service, and the State Revenue Service.

The Prime Minister, ministers, Ministers for Special Assignments, Deputy Prime Ministers, state ministers, office employees of the aforementioned officials (assistants, advisers, press secretaries) and parliamentary secretaries are not civil servants. In compliance with the paragraph 4 of Article 2 of the State Civil Service Law the norms of regulatory enactments regulating legal employment relations that prescribe the principle of equal rights, the prohibition of differential treatment principle, prohibition on causing adverse consequences, working hours and rest time, remuneration, the financial liability of employees and terms shall apply to the legal relations of the state civil service insofar as they are not prescribed by this law.[81] Consequently, the requirements of the Labour Law as in the private sector apply as regards collective the negotiation procedures also in the civil service. However, according to the Law on the Career Course of Service of Officials with Special Service Ranks Working in Institutions of the System of the Ministry of the Interior and the Prisons Administration, the norms of regulatory enactments regulating employment legal relationships are not applicable to officials, except the norms determining the periods, including limitation period, the prohibition of differential treatment, the term, type, and calculation of payment of work remuneration, the remuneration in cases when an employee does not work due to justifiable reasons, the deductions from work remuneration and limits thereof, the civil legal liability of an employee, the period of time which gives the right to annual paid leave, granting of prenatal and maternity leave, granting of leave to the father, adopter of the child or another person, and granting of parental leave, as well as the rights on pregnant women and breastfeeding women and women during the period following childbirth up to one year. (Article 3 of the Law).[82]

80. Article 3, http://www.vvc.gov.lv/export/sites/default/docs/LRTA/Likumi/State_Civil_Service_Law.doc, last visited 31 Dec. 2019.
81. http://www.vvc.gov.lv/export/sites/default/docs/LRTA/Likumi/State_Civil_Service_Law.doc, last visited 31 Dec. 2019.
82. http://www.likumi.lv, last visited 31 Dec. 2019.

Chapter 3. Historical Background

40. Latvia has been subject to continuous foreign rule since the thirteenth century (Germany, Poland, Lithuania, Russia, and Sweden). In the early medieval period inhabitants of the region resisted Christianization and became subject to attack in the Northern Crusades. Today's capital, Riga, founded in 1201 by Teutonic colonists at the mouth of the Daugava, became a strategic base in a papal-sanctioned conquest of the area by the Livonian Brothers of the Sword. It was to be the first major city of the southern Baltic and, after 1282, a principal trading centre in the Hanseatic League. The records of inhabitants of Latvia date back to the ancestors of Baltic Finns in around 3000 BC and the formation of the Baltic and Finno-Ugrian tribes in 2000 BC.

The territory of Latvia, through its access to the Baltic Sea trade routes, is strategically positioned. As a result, throughout the middle ages, Latvia (or parts of it) was controlled by other states, including Denmark, Poland-Lithuania, Sweden, and Russia. From the middle of the sixteenth century until the end of the eighteenth century, part of Latvia was known as the Duchy of Courland, a semi-independent state paying tribute to Poland.

In 1721, Russia took control of the Latvian territories following its victory over Sweden in the Great Northern War. In the 1860s, the Young Latvian Movement was formed in order to promote the indigenous language and oppose Russification policies and to counteract the socioeconomic oppression of Latvians. In 1903, the Latvian Social Democratic Union was formed, which continued to champion national interests and Latvia's national self-determination, particularly during the failed 1905 revolution in Russia.

Latvia was occupied by Germany during the First World War.[83] On 18 November 1918 – a few days after Germany surrendered to the Allies – Latvia declared its independence. Mr Kàrlis Ulmanis formed a government and was first Head of State but the hostilities between pro- and anti-Bolshevik forces continued until 1920, when Soviet Russia signed a peace treaty with the Parliamentary Republic of Latvia and recognized its independence in perpetuity. The international community (United Kingdom, France, Belgium, Italy, and Japan) recognized Latvia's independence on 26 January 1921. In April 1920 elections to the Constituent Assembly were held. On 22 September 1921, Latvia was admitted to the League of Nations. The Constitution (*Satversme*) was adopted in 1922. In June 1922, the new Law on Elections was passed, opening the way to electing *Saeima.*

41. In May 1934, the Prime Minister of Latvia Kàrlis Ulmanis took full power, banning all parties and many press organs, the activities of *Saeima* were suspended. On 23 August 1939, the Molotov–Ribbentrop Pact was signed between Germany and the Soviet Union. Its additional secret protocol placed Latvia under the Soviet sphere of influence. Soviet troops occupied the country on 17 June 1940 and staged elections were held on 14–15 July 1940. Nationalization and purges began, at least 35,000 inhabitants of Latvia being killed within one year. In 1941, Germany

83. *History of Latvia: the 20th century* (Riga: Jumava, 2006); *History of Latvia*: Outline, Spekke Arnolds (Riga: Jumava, 2006); *A History of Baltic States*, Kasekamp Andres (London, 2010).

invaded the USSR and occupied Latvia, until 8 May 1945, when Soviet control was re-established, and Latvia again experienced deportations and executions. After the war ended in 1945, Latvia was fully integrated into the centrally planned economic system of the Soviet Union. Soviet planners in Moscow pushed the growth of the heavy industry, and Latvia experienced rapid urbanization as people from across the USSR were resettled to work in its new factories.

42. In the late 1980s, as a result of Gorbachev's *glasnost* (openness) and *perestroika* (restructuring), an active mobilization for self-rule took place. In May 1990, the Supreme Council voted for independence following a transition period. Considering the unlawful nature of Latvia's annexation, Latvia continued to exist *de iure* as a subject of international law.

The pre-Second World War Constitution (*Satversme*) was reinstated. On 4 May 1990, Latvia regained its independence according to the Declaration on the restoration of independence of the Republic of Latvia on the grounds of state continuity. After the fall of the Soviet Union, the Supreme Council voted for the full restoration of Latvian independence, on 21 August 1991. Western countries and Russia recognized this, and Latvia joined the United Nations on 17 September 1991. The removal of the Russian Armed Forces (former USSR occupation forces) from Latvian territory was completed on 31 August 1994. The last remaining Russian military object in Latvia and the Baltic countries, the Skrunda Radar station (in western Latvia), ceased operations on 31 August 1998. On 21 October 1999, this final Russian military base in the Baltic States was handed over to the jurisdiction of Latvian authorities. A total of 850 former Soviet military installations in Latvia were destroyed in Latvia. In 2007, a border treaty between Latvia and Russia was signed and had subsequently been fully ratified by both states.

43. After achieving independence, Latvia sought to establish a free-market economy and reintegrate its economy with the rest of Europe. Toward this goal, Latvia quickly dismantled the Soviet economic structures and implemented comprehensive economic reforms to reduce government intervention in the economy and transfer public assets to the private sector. However, the economic transition was not smooth. The first difficulty was a severe shortage of fuels and raw materials, caused by the disruption of trading relationships resulting from the break-up of the Soviet Union. This forced Latvian enterprises to cut back or cease production, forcing many workers into unemployment. After a sharp decline GDP did not start growing again until 1994. In 1995 a banking crisis swept the country. Unwise loans and lax government supervision created conditions in which the nation's largest bank, Banka Baltija, and some of its smaller institutions failed and were unable to pay depositors the money they had entrusted to the bank. The government restored confidence by creating a stricter regulatory system to oversee banking practices. By the mid-1990s inflation was contained, and the national currency (Latvian Lats) was stable, both of which encouraged international trade and economic growth. With the renewal of independence, Latvia moved consistently towards two of its most important foreign policy goals – membership in the European Union and NATO. During the 1990s, many social, economic and judicial changes were implemented in order to prepare for admittance to these organizations.

44. Latvia was invited to begin negotiations to join the EU in 1997 and was formally invited to join at a summit in Copenhagen in December 2002. On the 27 December 2002, the Latvian Government decided to hold a referendum on the 20 September 2003 on joining the EU. In May 2003, the Parliament of Latvia amended the Constitution of Latvia to allow referendums on international matters, and the Latvian European Union membership referendum took place on 20 September 2003 to decide whether Latvia should join the European Union. Latvia was the last of the states, to join the EU in 2004 to hold a referendum on the issue. Just over two-thirds of voters voted 'yes' and Latvia joined the EU on 1 May 2004.[84]

45. The global economic crisis and breakdown in financial credit markets that led to recessions in several industrialised nations in 2008 had enormous repercussions in Latvia. Latvian banks, like their counterparts elsewhere, had invested heavily in so-called toxic mortgage securities. When the mortgage securities proved worthless and financial credit began to dry up, depositors in Latvia's second-largest bank, Parex Bank, started withdrawing their money, and the bank failed. In December 2008 the Latvian economy had to be rescued with a EUR 7.5 billion (USD 9.5 billion) loan package from the IMF, the World Bank, and the EU. The loan was conditioned on tax increases and cuts in government spending, leading to growing discontent with the government.

On 21 December 2011, Latvia concluded its three-year international loan programme during which the country implemented stringent austerity measures to stabilize its finances after the economic downturn.[85] According to the Prime Minister of Latvia Mr Valdis Dombrovskis, budget consolidation was an effective anti-crisis measure, while devaluation can be avoided and is not needed. On 9 July 2013 one of the largest international rating agencies Fitch Ratings has taken a decision to upgrade Latvia's credit rating by one level, establishing a stable rating future forecast.

By 31 March 2015, Latvia had repaid EUR 3.3 billion or 73.3% of the amount borrowed. As part of the financial assistance package, Latvia agreed to implement an economic reform programme whose principal objectives were to arrest the immediate liquidity crisis and then to restructure Latvia's economy and improve its competitiveness to reach sustainable GDP growth and a balanced budget as soon as practicable, while maintaining the exchange rate peg which was a key policy of both the Government and the Bank of Latvia in the period before the adoption of the euro. The programme included a range of measures to stabilise and strengthen the financial sector as well as substantial fiscal tightening to reduce financing needs and foster real depreciation.

84. The Central Election Commission of Latvia, http://www.cvk.gov.lv, last visited 31 Dec. 2019; EU referendum section by policy analysis portal, http://www.politika.lv/index.php?id=103834&lang=lv.
85. http://www.saeima.lv, last visited 15 Dec. 2019.

The economic reform programme also aimed to develop structural reforms and other policies to increase competitiveness and facilitate external adjustment, through tax incentives as well as improved property registration, construction approval and insolvency and liquidation processes. Close supervision of the financial sector and strengthening of banking regulations is continuing in Latvia, in line with EU directives.[86]

86. http://www.fm.gov.lv, last visited 15 Dec. 2019.

Chapter 4. Role of Government Institutions

§1. Degree of Government Intervention

46. According to the 2019 Index of Economic Freedom (an annual guide published by *The Wall Street Journal* and The Heritage Foundation, measured by determining the degree to which individuals are free to produce, distribute and consume goods and services) for Latvia is 70.4, making its economy the thirty-fifth freest in the 2019 Index.[87] Its score decreased by 3.2 points in comparison to 2018, reflecting declines in scores for judicial effectiveness, government integrity, and the tax burden far outweighing an improvement in fiscal health. Latvia is ranked 18th in the Europe region (forty-four countries), and its overall score is above the regional and world average. Latvia is now better positioned than many other countries in the region to sustain resilient economic growth.

In the World Bank's Doing Business 2018 report, Latvia was ranked 19th out of 190 countries on ease of doing business and 8th among the EU Member States.[88] Latvia continues to focus on improving the business environment. In Latvia, the Doing Business rating is used as a tool for reform assessment, which allows to highlighting the requirements where the administrative burden is too high, that is, it allows to compare the number and length of administrative procedures for their execution and related costs, as well as to assess the business environment as a whole.

47. In Latvia since the first years of regaining of independence, the state has played a significant role in setting the framework for industrial relations and labour law, incorporating, on the one hand, the legislator (new labour and social legislation, new rules for trade unions and employer organizations, legislative framework for collective bargaining, tripartite consultation and collective action) and on the other hand the employer.

§2. Incomes Policy

48. The Latvian taxation and duty system are governed by the Law on Taxes and Duties (adopted on 2 February 1995).[89] The Ministry of Finance is a responsible state institution for the development of state policy in the field of tax and customs administration. Tax payment supervision authority in Latvia is the State Revenue Service.[90] The tax and fee system in Latvia consists of: (a) state taxes, the object and rate of which are set by the *Saeima*; (b) state fees which shall be applicable according to the Law on Taxes and Fees, specific other laws and regulations of the Cabinet of Ministers; (c) local government fees which shall be applicable according to the Law on Taxes and Fees and binding regulations issued by the council of local

87. http://www.heritage.org/index/country/latvia, last visited 15 Dec. 2019.
88. Doing Business Report 2018, last visited 31 Dec. 2019.
89. http://likumi.lv/doc.php?id=33946, last visited 31 Dec. 2019.
90. The State Revenue Service, http://www.vid.gov.lv, last visited 31 Dec. 2019.

government; (d) directly applicable taxes and other obligatory payments set in the European Union regulatory enactments.[91] The following are direct and indirect taxes applicable in Latvia:

- *Personal income tax* – regulated by the Law on Personal Income Tax (to be paid by natural persons for their income); progressive personal income tax: for income up to EUR 20,004 – 20%; for income from EUR 20,004 to EUR 62,800 – 23%; for a part of income, exceeding EUR 62,800 – 31.4%). The tax is calculated and paid into the budget in two ways: in advance, also in the form of salary tax, and in accordance with the summary procedures, by drawing up an annual income declaration, also by way of a micro-enterprise tax and licence fees. Salary tax (income from employment, if a payroll tax book is submitted to the payer of income: 20% – for monthly income up to EUR 1,667; 23% – for a part of monthly income, exceeding EUR 1,667); 23% – (1) income from employment, if a payroll tax book is not submitted to the payer of income; (2) other income, if the payer pays both income subject to salary tax and other types of taxable income, for example, income from a contractor's agreement).[92]
- *Corporate income tax* – regulated by the Corporate Income Tax Law (effective as of 1 January 2018) and Cabinet Regulation No. 677 of 14 November 2017 'Regulations on the Application of Norms of the Corporate Income Tax Law'. Tax is paid by inland companies (including partnerships), institutions funded from the State or local government budget, the income of which from economic activities is not planned in the budget, permanent establishments and foreign businesses, as well as other foreign persons that gain income in Latvia. Tax is also paid by individual (family) companies (including farming and fishing enterprises), which prepare annual reports in accordance with the Law on Annual Reports and Consolidated Annual Reports. Tax is not paid by natural persons, societies, and foundations, religious organizations, trade unions, political parties, as well as private pension funds, investment funds, alternative investment funds, etc. The tax base is composed of distributed profit and deemed distributed profit. The following is considered to be distributed profit: calculated dividends, including extraordinary dividends; pay-outs equivalent to dividends; conditional dividends. The tax rate is 20% of the tax base; for non-residents – 3% and 20%, payments to persons in low-tax and zero-tax countries or territories – 20%. Tax is applied to the tax base, which includes taxable objects: (1) distributed profit; (2) conditionally distributed profit. When assessing the corporate income tax base, the value of taxable objects is divided by the coefficient 0.8. The taxation period is a month.
- *Real estate tax* – regulated by the Law on Immovable Property Tax (to be paid by real estate owners or legal possessors). The tax on immovable property is assessed on the cadastral value of the object of immovable property tax at 1 January of the taxation year. If the object of immovable property tax has been registered in the Public Information System of immovable property within the taxation year, the tax is assessed on the cadastral value of the tax object at the moment of

91. www.likumi.lv, last visited 31 Dec. 2019.
92. https://likumi.lv/ta/en/en/id/56880-on-personal-income-tax, last visited 31 Dec. 2019.

registration. Tax rates: land – 1,5% of the cadastral value; buildings used for economic activity, engineering structures – 1.5% of the cadastral value; residential buildings, apartments – 0.2%–0.6% (0.2% of the cadastral value not exceeding EUR 56,915; 0.4% of the part of the cadastral value exceeding EUR 56,915, but less than EUR 106,715; 0.6% of the cadastral value exceeding EUR 106,715). An additional 1.5% tax rate is applicable for uncultivated agricultural land, excluding land that has an area less than one hectare. Special 3% tax rate is applicable for collapsed constructions, constructions degrading the environment or threatening the safety of individuals if it is determined by the municipality in its binding regulations. The tax base for collapsed object is the highest value of the building or the land, on which the building is located (because the market value for ruins are '0').The local governments notify the payer or maintenance manager of an apartment house of the amount of immovable property tax in the current taxation (calendar) year by sending to them or persons authorised by them by 15 February of the same year the payment order at the indicated address. The time for sending out tax payment notices for unfarmed agricultural land is 15 February of the subsequent taxation year. The immovable property tax must be paid once in a quarter – no later than on 31 March, 15 May, 15 August, and 15 November – in the amount of one-quarter of the annual amount of the tax. The tax can also be paid in advance once a year.[93]

- *Value-added tax* – regulated by the Value Added Tax Law (to be paid by legal entities and natural persons; the standard tax rate is 21%, reduced tax rate (zero; 5% or 12%).[94]
- *Excise duty* (to be applied to oil products, natural gas, alcoholic drinks, beer, tobacco products, coffee and non-alcoholic drinks, liquid to be used in electronic cigarettes).[95]
- *Customs duty* – regulated by the Customs Law (to be paid by natural persons and legal entities when importing goods into the EU).[96]
- *Raffle/lottery and gambling tax* – regulated by the Raffle and Gambling Tax Law (to be paid by lottery and gambling providers).[97]
- *State social insurance compulsory contribution* – regulated by the Law on State Social Insurance (a compulsory insurance contribution is a compulsory payment specified by law into the account of a special budget, which gives the right to a socially insured person to receive social insurance services prescribed by law; shall be paid by insured persons and their employers. The total rate is 34.09% which varies for different categories of insured persons (11% tax rate for employee and 24.09% tax rate for an employer). From 1 January 2018 maximum amount of the object of the State social insurance mandatory contributions is EUR 55,000 per year.[98]
- *Micro-enterprise tax* – regulated by the Microenterprise Tax Law (adopted on 9 August 2010). A micro-enterprise tax rate for a micro-enterprise turnover up to

93. *Ibid.*
94. *Ibid.*
95. *Ibid.*
96. *Ibid.*
97. *Ibid.*
98. *Ibid.*

EUR 40,000 is 15%, if a micro-enterprise taxpayer does not exceed the designated criteria. If the micro-enterprise did not have a turnover in the taxation period (calendar year) or the calculated amount of the micro-enterprise tax does not exceed EUR 50, a micro-enterprise taxpayer shall pay the micro-enterprise tax into the budget in the amount of EUR 50. Micro-enterprise tax includes: state social insurance mandatory contributions, personal income tax and State fee of the business risk for micro-enterprise employees, enterprise income tax, if the micro-enterprise conforms to the features of the enterprise income taxpayer, personal income tax of the micro-enterprise owner for the part of the micro-enterprise revenue from the economic activity. Tax replaces state social insurance contributions both for employees and proprietors and business risk state fee as well as personal income tax or corporate income tax depending on legal form of taxpayer. The legal form of micro-enterprise could be a limited liability company or an individual merchant or individual performing economic activity without registration as an individual merchant. To qualify for status of micro-enterprise taxpayer the following criteria shall be met: turnover does not exceed EUR 40,000 per year, the number of employees may not exceed five).[99]

– *Electricity tax* – regulated by the Electricity Tax Law (to be paid by persons supplying electricity to the end-users and self-governing producers). The tax rate is set in EUR per megawatt-hour.[100]
– *Tax on cars and motorcycles* – regulated by the Law on the Vehicle Operation Tax and Company Car Tax (tax shall be paid when the car or motorcycle is registered in Latvia for the first time).[101]
– *Company car tax*– regulated by the Law on the Vehicle Operation Tax and Company Car Tax (this is paid by commercial entities and foreign merchant branch who own or hold passenger vehicle or truck with the total weight up to 3,000 kg and which have more than three seats (including the driver's seat) and which is used also for personal needs of employees and/or proprietors).[102]
– *Vehicle operating tax*-regulated by the Law on the Vehicle Operation Tax and Company Car Tax (to be paid by legal entities and natural persons who own, possess or hold a vehicle, which is registered or is going to be registered in Latvia, or whose owned, possessed or held vehicle is given transit number plates).
– *Natural resources tax* (to be paid by legal entities and natural persons if extracting natural resources, distributing or importing environmentally unfriendly goods or which are allowed to perform such activities).[103]
– *Solidarity tax* (a taxable object is income, which exceeds a maximum amount of the object of the State social insurance mandatory contributions). Taxpayers are employees, employer, and self-employed persons. From 1 January 2018 until 31 December 2018 taxable object is income above EUR 55,000 per year. As from 1 January 2019 taxable object is income above EUR 62,800 per year. Tax rate until

99. *Ibid.*
100. *Ibid.*
101. *Ibid.*
102. *Ibid.*
103. *Ibid.*

31 December 2018 is the same as the State social insurance mandatory contributions' rate. If an employee has been insured for all types of social insurance than rate is 35.09% (11% tax rate for employee and 24.09% tax rate for employer). Tax rate differs for those taxpayers who are insured not for all types of social insurance (e.g., self-employed persons, pensioners). As from 1 January 2019 tax rate is 25.50%.

49. According to the Section 159 of the Latvian Administrative Violations Code on evasion of taxes and payments imposed together therewith, as well as the concealment (reduction) of income, profit or other taxable objects – a fine shall be imposed on natural persons or to an amount from EUR 40 to EUR 2,100, subtracting a board member the right to hold certain positions in commercial companies or not. If an employer has not paid compulsory contributions to the state social insurance to the budget to the full amount, the provisions of Article 32 of the Law on Taxes and Fees shall be applied.[104] If a taxpayer in violating requirements of tax laws reduces the tax amount to be paid into the budget, the tax administration shall assess the tax audit and recover from a taxpayer for the benefit of the budget the reduced tax amount, late interest payment and a fine which is set according to this law, unless specific tax laws provide for a different fine amount. If the amount a taxpayer should pay into the budget for the period for which the tax audit has been carried out is reduced by not more than 15% of the declared amount, the fine shall be set at the amount of 20% of the undeclared tax amount to be paid into the budget.

If the amount a taxpayer should pay into the budget for the period for which the tax audit has been carried out is reduced by more than 15% of the declared amount, the fine should be set in the amount of 30% of the undeclared tax amount to be paid into the budget.

When an employer has missed a deadline for paying the compulsory contributions, Article 16(2) of the Law on State Social Insurance[105] shall be applied which determines that for missing the deadline for paying the compulsory contributions late interest payments shall be recovered from the timely unpaid amount of mandatory contributions (principle debt) for each day delayed according to the Law on Taxes and Fees.

If an employer employs an employee without entering into agreement, or pays an employee a salary which exceeds the amount indicated in official documents (accounting records and reports to the State Revenue Service), that is, the so called 'envelope salary', Article 16^1 of the Law on State Social Insurance shall be applied.

According to Paragraph 1 of Article 16^1 of the above-mentioned law, if an employer has employed or employs a person without entering into an employment, work-performance or carriage agreement, and an employer has assessed or paid, or had to assess and pay, an employee an income from which compulsory contributions had to be assessed but this income is not presented in accounting records and in the report to the State Revenue Service on compulsory state social insurance contributions from employees' labour income, personal income tax and the entrepreneur risk state fee in the reporting month submitted to the State Revenue Service

104. http://www.likumi.lv, last visited 31 Dec. 2019.
105. *Ibid.*

and from which no compulsory contributions were assessed, the tax administration shall recover from an employer compulsory contributions and fines in the amount of three times the compulsory contributions from the amount which corresponds to amount paid to a person, if it is possible to determine and if it exceeds the minimum wage set by the Cabinet of Ministers, or to the minimum wage set by the Cabinet of Ministers if the actual amount equals or is less than it, or if the actual amount is impossible to determine.

According to Paragraph 1^1 of Article 16^1 of the Law on State Social Insurance if an employer has employed or employs a person entering into an employment, work-performance or carriage agreement but the income paid from which compulsory contributions had to be assessed is not presented in the accounting records, in the report on compulsory state social insurance contributions from employees' labour income, personal income tax and the entrepreneur risk state fee in the reporting month submitted to the State Revenue Service and from which no compulsory contributions were assessed, the State Revenue Service shall recover from an employer compulsory contributions from the amount which corresponds to actual amount paid to a person and a fine in the amount of three times the compulsory contributions.

According to Paragraph 3 of Article 16^1 of the above-mentioned Law if it is determined that an employer employed a person without entering into employment, work-performance or carriage agreement but it is impossible for the tax administration to identify the person employed compulsory contributions shall be recovered in the procedure provided for in Paragraph 1 of this article without naming particular persons.

According to Paragraph 5 of Article 16^1 of the Law on State Social Insurance if for the persons referred to in Article 1(2)(a) of this Law an employer assessed compulsory contributions from salary which is lower than the minimum wage set by the Cabinet of Ministers and there are no justification documents confirming it, the tax administration shall recover from an employer compulsory contributions and a fine in the amount of three times the mandatory contributions from the amount corresponding to the amount of minimum wage set by the Cabinet of Ministers.

50. Latvia has a statutory national minimum wage, set directly by the Cabinet of Ministers after tripartite consultations with main employers' organizations and trade unions. Article 107 of the Constitution of the Republic of Latvia provides that 'Every employed person has the right to receive, for work done, commensurate remuneration which shall not be less than the minimum wage established by the State'. Article 61 of the Labour Law sets the main provisions regarding minimum wage. In compliance with the Labour Law, a minimum wage must not be less than the minimum level determined by the State. The minimum monthly salary within the scope of normal working time, as well as minimum hourly wage rates, is determined by the Cabinet of Ministers. The Cabinet of Ministers determines the procedures for the specification and review of the minimum monthly wage in Regulation No. 563 as of August 2016. The minimum wage is a constant subject for debate and one of the main social dialogue issues. The term 'minimum income' is not defined in labour legislation; instead, various minimum income indicators for different purposes are used in Latvia, e.g. the statistical value of the minimum consumer basket of goods and services per capita. Since 1 January 2018, the amount of minimum wage has been EUR 430 per month. Every year the Ministry of Welfare together with the Ministry of Finance and the Ministry of Economics shall asses the economic situation in the State and develop proposals for the amount of minimum monthly salary. For discussions the economic situation in Latvia should be evaluated every year by analysing the macroeconomic forecasts prepared by the Ministry of Economics and the Ministry of Finance of Latvia and by analysing changes in the economic situation during the previous year, the macroeconomic forecasts prepared by the Ministry of Economics and the Ministry of Finance, and changes in the economic situation in the previous year, including the development of labour productivity; the information at the disposal of the State Revenue Service regarding the average labour income of employees and the number of hours worked per month in the previous calendar year according to the information indicated in employer reports on the mandatory State social insurance contributions from the labour income of employees, personal income tax and State duty of the business risk in the reporting month; the assessment conducted by the Ministry of Welfare of the impact on social security and tax burden of labour force, including with regard to the changes in the object of the mandatory State social insurance contributions of employee and employer in the reporting month; the information provided by the SEA on the unemployment rate divided by cities and municipalities of the Republic; the proportion of the minimum monthly salary to the average work remuneration in the State in the previous year calculated by the Central Statistical Bureau; the labour cost index calculated by the Central Statistical Bureau (against the relevant period of the previous year); the proposals developed by the Ministry of Finance for changes in the tax system for the following year (changes in the personal income tax rate, the minimum not subject to the personal income tax, and amount of relief for a dependant); the assessment conducted by the Ministry of Welfare of the amount of the existing minimum monthly gross and net salary and its possible changes in the following year in other European Union Member States, as well as the comparison of the proportion of the minimum monthly salary to the minimum work remuneration in those countries; the proposals developed by the Ministry of Welfare for changes in rates of the mandatory State social insurance contributions for the following year; the proportion calculated by the Central Statistical Bureau: the number of the employees whose work remuneration is equal to or smaller than the amount of the minimum monthly salary to the total number of employees. Estimates will consider any proposed changes in the monthly minimum wage, as well as any planned changes in tax thresholds in the neighbouring Baltic states of Estonia and Lithuania.

§3. Competence of Ministries and Agencies in Labour Questions

51. The Ministry of Welfare is the leading actor in the field of labour law and industrial relations. The mission of the Ministry of Welfare is to stabilize the condition of a person in the situations of social risk, to reduce the possibility that the social risk would occur by facilitating decent legal labour relationships, healthy and safe work conditions, gender equality thus creating the opportunities to everybody to secure a sufficient life quality themselves in any given situation.[106]

The SLI was established by the Law on Labour Inspectorate,[107] it is the main institution responsible for supervision and monitoring of the implementation of labour legislation in Latvia. The officials of the Inspectorate have the right to:

- carry out examinations, control and investigation at the undertakings;
- request the information necessary in order to verify that the requirements of labour legislation are observed;
- take decisions regarding matters of legal employment relationships and to issue warnings and orders to employers;
- impose, by the procedures prescribed for the examination of administrative violations, administrative sanctions on employers.

Among its functions is the monitoring of compliance with the legislation regulating employment relations and the observance of the rights of employees. The functions of the SLI are as follows:

- to supervise and control implementation of the requirements of normative acts on employment relations and health and safety at work;
- to control the fulfilment of the mutual obligations of employers and employees imposed by employment contracts and collective agreements;
- to promote cooperation of employers and employees and to carry out measures to facilitate the resolution of disputes between employer and employees;
- to perform the investigation and uniform registration of accidents at work and to participate in investigation of the cases of occupational diseases according to the procedure stipulated by normative acts;
- to control equipment at workplaces, use of personal and collective protective equipment of the staff, use of harmful and dangerous substances, as well observance of technological processes according to the requirements of normative acts;
- to provide free of charge consultations to employers and employees on the requirements of normative acts in the field of employment legal relations and health and safety at work labour;
- to organize the establishment of the national Focal Point of the European Agency for Safety and Health at Work and to ensure its operation.

The legal framework of the occupational safety and health protection system is set up by the Labour Protection Law[108] adopted on 20 June 2001 and is in force since 1 January 2002. The Labour Protection Law transposes the requirements and principles of the EU Framework Directive on Safety and Health at Work.

---

106. The Ministry of Welfare of the Republic of Latvia, http://www.lm.gov.lv, last visited 31 Dec. 2019.
107. http://www.likumi.lv, last visited 31 Dec. 2019.
108. *Ibid.*

52. The Latvian Administrative Violations Code[109] regulates in the Chapter V on Administrative Violations in the Protection of Labour and Citizens Health sanctions in cases of violations of employment legislation.

For violation of the regulatory enactments regulating employment legal relations:[110]

- in the case of not entering into a written form of the contract of employment a fine shall be imposed on the employer for a natural person in an amount from EUR 70 up to EUR 350,[111] and for a legal person from EUR 700 up to EUR 3,600;
- in the case of not ensuring the state specified minimum monthly wage, if the person is employed for a normal working time, or not ensuring the minimal hourly tariff rates, a fine shall be imposed on the employer for a natural person or an official in an amount from EUR 430 up to EUR 570, and for a legal person from EUR 850 up to EUR 7,100;
- in the case of not entering into a written form of the contract of employment, if the violations have been recommitted within a year after the imposition of administrative sanction – a fine should be imposed on the employer for a natural person or an official in an amount from EUR 350 up to EUR 700, and for a legal person from EUR 3,600 up to EUR 7,100;
- in the cases of the violations provided for in paragraph 2 of this article (non-concluding of written contract of employment), if they have been recommitted within a year after the imposition of administrative sanction a fine should be imposed on the employer for a natural person or an official in an amount from EUR 350 up to EUR 700, and for a legal person from EUR 3,600 up to EUR 7,100;
- in the cases of the violations provided for in Paragraph 3 of this article (non-payment of minimum monthly wage), if they have been recommitted within a year after the imposition of administrative sanction a fine should be imposed on the employer for a natural person or an official in an amount from EUR 570 up to EUR 700), and for a legal person from EUR 7,100 up to EUR 14,000.

53. For conclusion of a contract of employment with an employee, whose knowledge of the official language is inadequate to fulfil professional and work duties thereof and who has not produced the document provided for in regulatory enactments that certifies knowledge of the official language (Article 41^1):[112]

- in the case of a conclusion of a contract of employment with an employee, whose knowledge of the official language is inadequate to fulfil professional and work duties thereof and who has not produced a document provided for in regulatory enactments of the Republic of Latvia which certifies knowledge of the official language, if the regulatory enactment requires knowledge of the official language

109. *Ibid.*
110. *Ibid.*
111. *Ibid.*
112. *Ibid.*

in order to fulfil the relevant duties a fine should be imposed on the employer or the official from EUR 140 up to EUR 350;
- in the case of violations provided for in Paragraph 1 of this section, if they have been recommitted within a year after the imposition of administrative sanction – a fine should be imposed on the official or the employer – for a natural person from EUR 280 up to EUR 700, for an employer – for a legal person from EUR 700 up to EUR 1,400.

54. For violation of the right to strike (Article 41^2):[113]

- in the case of an employee, who does not participate in a strike, who is compelled to perform the work of striking employees, as well as the recruitment of employees in place of the striking employees, in order to prevent or stop the strike or delay the implementation of the striking workers' claims a fine should be imposed the employer – for a natural person or an official in the amount from EUR 140 up to EUR 350, and for a legal person from EUR 350 up to EUR 700;
- in the case of inviting others to participate in an illegal strike as a result of which a strike occurs, a fine should be imposed on the employees or trade union leaders from EUR 140 up to EUR 350;
- in the case of continuing an illegal strike – a fine should be imposed on the trade union leaders in an amount from EUR 140 up to EUR 350.

55. For violation of information and consultation requirements in European Community-wide commercial companies, European Community commercial company groups and the violation of the requirements regarding the involvement of workers in European commercial companies (Article 41^3):[114]

- in the case of the disclosure of confidential information to a third party, which has been obtained whilst working in the European Works Council, within special discussion groups or other groups for the information and consultation of employees, or the disclosure of information containing commercial secrets to a third party in the case of the establishment of a European company, which has been obtained while working within a special discussion group, representative committee or within any other procedures for employees' information, consultation and participation a fine in an amount from EUR 140 up to EUR 350 should be imposed;
- in the case of failure to provide information to employees or their representatives regarding the number of employees in a European Community-wide commercial company group or failure to provide information to employees or their representatives regarding commercial companies established by the European commercial companies or dependent companies, and the number of employees employed in these companies, and in the field of the involvement of employees in the decision making process in the commercial companies' current activities a fine in an amount up to EUR 7,100 should be imposed on the employer;

113. *Ibid.*
114. *Ibid.*

- in the case of failure to compensate the establishment or operational expenditure of the European Works Council or a special discussion group in a European Community-wide commercial company or the European Community commercial company group or in the case of failure to compensate the establishment or operational expenditure of a special discussion group or representative committee in a European commercial company – a fine in an amount up to EUR 7,100 should be imposed on the employer;
- in the case of failure to provide a report at least once a year to the European Works Council regarding the commercial development and prospects of a European Community commercial company or the European Community commercial company group or in the case of failure to provide a report at least once a year to a representative committee regarding the commercial activity and further development of a European commercial company – a fine in an amount up to EUR 7,100 should be imposed on the employer;
- in the case of failure to inform a European Works Council committee or, in its absence, the European Works Council of special circumstances, which substantially affects workers' interests in a European Community-wide commercial company or European Community commercial company group, or in the case of failure to inform a representative committee of special circumstances, which substantially affect workers' interests in a European commercial company – a fine in an amount up to EUR 7,100 should be imposed on the employer.

56. For violation of the regulatory enactments regulating labour protection (Article 41(4)):[115]

- in the case of violation of the regulatory enactments that regulate labour protection, except for the violations referred to in Paragraphs 2, 3, 4, 5 and 6 of this Article a warning should be issued or a fine should be imposed on the employer or user undertaking[116] for a natural person or an official in an amount from EUR 70 up to EUR 350, and for a legal person – from EUR 70 up to EUR 700;
- in the case of non-performance of a work environment risk assessment and the non-development of a labour protection measures plan or the non-conformity thereof with the requirements of regulatory enactments regulating labour protection – a warning should be issued or a fine should be imposed on the employer or user undertaking – for a natural person or an official in an amount from EUR 70 up to EUR 350, and for a legal person – from EUR 140 up to EUR 1,100;
- in the case of not using safety signs and not placing them appropriately in the work environment a fine should be imposed on the employer or user undertaking for a natural person or an official in an amount from EUR 70 up to EUR 350, and for a legal person – from EUR 140 up to EUR 700;
- in the case of not sending employees for the performance of mandatory health examinations, if such are provided for in regulatory enactments a warning should be issued or a fine should be imposed on the employer or user undertaking for a

115. *Ibid.*
116. User undertaking – any natural or legal person for whom and under the supervision and direction of whom a temporary agency worker works temporarily.

natural person or an official in an amount from EUR 70 up to EUR 350, and for a legal person from EUR 140 up to EUR 700;
- in the case of failure to investigate an accident at work in conformity with the requirements of regulatory enactments or its concealment a fine should be imposed on the employer or user undertaking for a natural person or an official in an amount from EUR 140 up to EUR 500, and for a legal person from EUR 350 up to EUR 1,400;
- in the case of failure to investigate an accident at work in conformity with the requirements of regulatory enactments or its concealment, as a result of which the employee has been caused serious health disorders or his or her death has occurred a fine should be imposed on the employer or user undertaking for a natural person or an official in an amount from EUR 500 up to EUR 700, and for a legal person from EUR 2,100 up to EUR 4,300;
- in the cases of the violations provided for in paragraph 1, 2, 3, 4 and 5 of this article, if they have been recommitted within a year after the imposition of administrative sanction a fine should be imposed on the employer or user undertaking for a natural person or an official in an amount from EUR 500 up to EUR 700, and for a legal person from EUR 1,400 up to EUR 2,900;
- in the case of the violations provided for in Paragraph six of this article, if they have been recommitted within a year after the imposition of administrative sanction – a fine should be imposed on the employer or user undertaking – for a natural person or an official in an amount from EUR 570 up to EUR 700, and for a legal person – from EUR 5,700 up to EUR 14,000.

57. For violation of the regulatory enactments regulating labour protection that cause a direct threat to the safety and health of employees (Article 41(5)):[117]

- in the case of violation of regulatory enactments that regulate labour protection, which cause a direct threat to the safety and health of an employee, except the violations referred to in Paragraphs two, three and four of this article – a fine should be imposed on the employer or user undertaking – for a natural person or an official in an amount from EUR 500 up to EUR 700, and for a legal person – from EUR 1,400 up to EUR 2,900;
- in the case of not ensuring employees with personal means of protection necessary for work which cause a direct threat to the safety and health of an employee – a fine should be imposed on the employer or user undertaking – for a natural person or an official in an amount from EUR 350 up to EUR 700, and for a legal person – from EUR 1,400 up to EUR 2,900;
- in the case of using work equipment not in conformity with the requirements of regulatory enactments regulating labour protection or non-observance of safety requirements which cause a direct threat to the safety and health of an employee – a fine should be imposed on the employer or user undertaking – for a natural person or an official in an amount from EUR 350 up to EUR 700, and for a legal person – from EUR 1,400 up to EUR 2,900;

117. http://www.likumi.lv, last visited 22 Dec. 2016.

- in the case of failing to instruct employees or the non-performance of training on issues regarding the safety and health of employees at work which cause a direct threat to the safety and health of an employee – a fine should be imposed on the employer or user undertaking – for a natural person or an official in an amount from EUR 350 up to EUR 700, and for a legal person – from EUR 1,400 up to EUR 2,900;
- in cases of the violations provided for in Paragraph 1, 2, 3 and 4 of this article, if they have been recommitted within a year after the imposition of administrative sanction a fine should be imposed on the employer or user undertaking for a natural person or an official in an amount from EUR 570 up to EUR 700, and for a legal person – from EUR 4,300 up to EUR 14,000.

58. For provision of labour protection services violating the requirements specified for competent specialists and competent institutions in the regulatory enactments regulating labour protection (Article 41(6)):[118]

- in the case of the provision of labour protection services, including risk assessment, violating the requirements specified for competent specialists and competent institutions in regulatory enactments, or in the case of the provision of labour protection services without a competent specialist certificate or a competent institution quality system certificate a fine should be imposed for a natural person in an amount from EUR 350 up to EUR 700, and for a legal person from EUR 1,400 up to EUR 4,300;
- in the case of not performing internal supervision of the work environment in conformity with regulatory enactments regulating labour protection, including risk assessment, or the violation of the requirements specified for competent specialists and competent institutions in regulatory enactments a fine should be imposed for a natural person in an amount from EUR 140 up to EUR 350, and for a legal person – from EUR 700 up to EUR 1,400;
- in the case of not performing internal supervision of the work environment in conformity with regulatory enactments regulating labour protection, including risk assessment, or the violation of the requirements specified for competent specialists and competent institutions in regulatory enactments, which cause a direct threat to the safety and health of an employee a fine should be imposed for a natural person in an amount from EUR 500 up to EUR 700, and for a legal person – from EUR 1,400 up to EUR 4,300;
- in the case of violations provided for in this section, if they have been recommitted within a year after the imposition of administrative sanction a fine should be imposed for a natural person in an amount from EUR 570 up to EUR 700, and for a legal person from EUR 4,300 up to EUR 7,100.

In few cases, foreseen in the Criminal Law of Latvia,[119] criminal sanctions may be imposed upon the employer by the respective criminal courts.

118. *Ibid.*
119. *Ibid.*

59. According to Paragraph 1 of Article 3 of the SLI Law, the primary function of the SLI is the implementation of state supervision and control in the field of employment legal relationships and labour protection.

60. The Report on 2018 activities of SLI shows statistics regarding violations – Violations of regulatory enactments regulating the labour relations made up 31% of all violations detected by the officials of the Labour Inspectorate in 2018. Ninety-seven per cent of violations of the labour relations formed violations of the Labour Law (79%) and Regulations on Registration of Persons Making Mandatory State Social Insurance Contributions and Reports on Mandatory State Social Insurance Contributions and Personal Income Tax (18%). In 2018, as in previous years, most employers did not comply with the requirements of the Labour Law regarding employment contract, which were 30% of all labour relations violations. The violations found were related to having a written employment contract and the content of the contract. A significant part of the Labour Law violations was related to the termination of employment relationships. Implementation of the 'Consult First' principle in practice in 2018 was the horizontal priority of the Labour Inspectorate penetrating all activity areas of the Labour Inspectorate completely: both when carrying inspections of companies and when performing a broad public information and education work. In 2018, 1,198 unregistered persons were identified, of whom 666 persons had not signed written employment contracts and were not declared at the SRS; 362 had written employment contracts but were not registered at the SRS, and 170 persons did not enter into written employment contracts but were declared at the SRS. In 2018, discovering the employment without a written employment contract and /or declaration at the SRS, the officials of the Labour Inspectorate imposed 707 fines in the amount of EUR 463,130 on the basis of the Latvian Administrative Violations Code.

61. The SEA carries out the implementation of the national employment policy, including the provision of labour market services and it is a state administration institution under the supervision of the Ministry for Welfare.[120] The SEA implements the state policy in the area of unemployment reduction and the field of support for unemployed persons, jobseekers and persons subject to the risk of unemployment.[121]

The competence of the SEA according to the Law on Support to Unemployed Persons and Job Seekers covers as well as registration, placement, training and re-training of unemployed persons.[122] The set of measures for unemployed and also employed persons is aimed at promoting inclusive labour market by providing appropriate training and educational programmes, as well as other services (for example, vocational guidance) in order to better match persons' knowledge and experience with labour market needs.[123]

120. Law on Support to Unemployed and Jobseekers; http://www.vvc.gov.lv; last visited 15 Dec. 2019.
121. The State Employment agency, http://www.nva.gov.lv, last visited 15 Dec. 2019.
122. http://www.likumi.lv, last visited 31 Dec. 2019.
123. The Ministry of Welfare, http://www.lm.gov.lv, last visited 31 Dec. 2019.

In pre-crisis years, when the unemployment rate in Latvia was low, the main challenges for the labour market were to enhance labour competitiveness and to promote the inclusion of marginalised groups into the labour market. Taking into account the severe consequences of the global crisis and the impact of the macroeconomic adjustment and reforms, there was a need for both types of measures – short-term measures, aimed at reducing the risk of increased poverty and economic inactivity (public works programmes, complex inclusion measures, training for employed, training vouchers for unemployed with unfinished tertiary education) and long-term measures, aimed at enhancing labour force competitiveness and giving positive signals to unemployed and other people in general. After this the focus has been put on more individualized support to unemployed looking at obstacles to labour market participation, enhancing job search support and outreach activities and implementing a profiling system as well as measures for improving labour market transparency including a more effective CV and vacancies portal. Additionally, the evidence base has been strengthened for active labour market policies by carrying out high-quality impact evaluations.[124]

On the request of employers, the SEA offers training for unemployed. The SEA covers all costs associated with the training of unemployed. An employer may request the SEA:

- to train unemployed persons for the needs of an undertaking in any educational programme;
- to participate in the selection of unemployed persons for the training;
- to train specified unemployed persons in particular occupations necessary for an employer;
- to participate in qualification exams and to choose employees from those unemployed persons and jobseekers who have completed the training programme;

Employers may offer practice places for educational institutions in order to assess the skills of potential employees in the actual working environment and to allow an applicant to obtain the necessary skills at a particular workplace.

The SEA through its network of regional offices provides career guidance advice and counselling free of charge to jobseekers, the employed and persons in education or planning to return to education that requires information or support to achieve their career goals. Unemployed persons and jobseekers registered with the SEA can choose group or individual career and/or counselling, career guidance, identification of suitable employment goals, job search information, assistance, and retraining. Individuals are offered interest, aptitude, personality and psychometric testing, health profiling, role play, coaching and information provision. Group activities involve consultations, seminars and lectures on career management issues, career motivation tests and interpersonal communication training. SEA internet services include online career interest tests, information on careers and training opportunities, storage of CV, motivation letters, as well as responses to user questions by career guidance and/or counsellors.

124. The Ministry of Welfare, Report on Labour Market, http://www.lm.gov.lv, last visited 31 Dec. 2019.

I. Placement and Job-Search Assistance

62. The SEA registers vacancies submitted by employers and carries out the placement of unemployed and persons seeking employment, helping them to integrate into the labour market. The SEA records and informs about the vacant workplaces, organizes cooperation and information exchange between employers and unemployed persons, implements and administers ALMP measures, provides consultation on occupational suitability, selection of an appropriate occupation and vocational training, issues licences and supervises legal persons who provide work placement services etc.

II. Vocational Training, Requalification, Qualification Improvement and Non-formal Training

63. This includes different training programs (continuing vocational training to acquire a vocational qualification, advanced vocational training to reach vocational proficiency, non-formal and on-the-job training) organized in cooperation with educational institutions and employers. Since 2011, the training of unemployed and job-seekers is implemented by applying the method of training vouchers. Training fields and educational programmes are organized in accordance with the labour market demand and national economy development forecasts and agreed with economic and social partners and experts. The length of training programmes may vary from 60 to 160 hours for non-formal training programmes to 320/480/960/1120/1280 hours for vocational training programmes. Simple or low-skilled occupations are excluded from the list of training programmes. The following activity also is carried out within the measure – if an employer cannot find an appropriate employee in the labour market, he may request the SEA to select and train an unemployed person for him. Within the activity, an employer is responsible for providing on-the-job training and is obliged to provide a workplace after the training is finished. On-the-job training is also organized for unemployed with an obsolete qualification or without a document, certifying the proficiency of a person. Participants are also receiving financial support during training – monthly training allowance. The following additional expenses are also covered from the state budget: wage supplements for supervisors during on-the-job training, training, or working place adaptation for persons with disability, the involvement of different experts, such as assistants, signs language experts, etc.

III. Measures to Enhance Competitiveness

64. These include different short courses, seminars, lectures and consultations offered to unemployed in areas such as communications skills, networking, negotiation, job-finding and interview skills, motivation. These measures are aimed mainly to improve social and functional skills and to provide psychological support, basic skills and abilities necessary for the labour market, as well as an acquisition of work finding techniques and non-formal education programmes, including knowledge of the state official language, as well as many other activities, facilitating the competitiveness of unemployed and persons seeking employment in the labour market.

IV. Career Counselling and Vocational Guidance

65. This includes help in career planning, provides professional suitability tests and acquisition of work finding and maintaining techniques. Vocational counselling and career guidance services are offered to all unemployed and jobseekers. The services include consultations on choosing education and career, vocational development, returning to the labour market and changing occupations, assessment of client's vocational aptitude, interests and preferences, abilities, skills and suitability for a given profession, consultations about effective ways of searching for a work, provision of information about the content and requirements of different occupations, information about educational and training opportunities in Latvia and abroad.

V. Subsidized Employment for the Most Vulnerable Groups of Unemployed

66. This includes different projects aimed at specific target groups of unemployed – persons with disability, youth, older workers, long-term unemployed, young parents after child leave, etc. The aim of the measure is to facilitate the development of sustainable and long-term working places for unemployed. Usually, financial support is provided for a maximum period of twelve to twenty-four months for unemployed with disability and includes monthly wage subsidy which equals to the amount of minimum monthly wage. The following additional expenses are also covered from the state budget: wage supplements for supervisors during on-the-job training, training or working place adaptation for persons with disability, involvement of different experts, such as assistants, mentors, silent language experts, etc.

VI. Measures to Support the Unemployed to Enter Self-Employment or Entrepreneurship

67. These include training programmes, consultations and grants for business start-up or self-employment. Support is provided to unemployed with an appropriate level of knowledge, who have gained a sufficient level of education or completed vocational training or non-formal education programmes in the SEA (different training courses in business administration, for example, basics of business administration, project management, business plan developing, accounting and finance, marketing and basic management), as well as for those, who have already developed their business plans and wish to take practical consultations regarding implementation. The financial support is provided for the development, evaluation, and implementation of a business plan.

VII. Lifelong Learning Programmes

68. The unemployed persons can receive coupons and participate in professional further education programmes allowing them to acquire professional qualification. After completing a particular programme, the unemployed person is required to take an examination. After passing the examination, the unemployed person receives a professional qualification certificate. Fields of training and professions for an unemployed person and jobseeker training are determined by a commission established by the Ministry of Welfare in accordance with labour market demand and national economy development forecasts. An unemployed person may choose an education programme and establishment from the list of Fields of training and professions approved by the Ministry of Welfare. An unemployed person may choose a further professional education or professional vocational development programme and education establishment form the list of the professional further education or professional vocational development programmes offered by SEA or choose the education establishment on their own. An unemployed person receives a coupon for acquiring the chosen education programme. An unemployed person with disability may obtain specific professional education programmes online. The training period is up to 8 months. During the training, unemployed persons are provided with a monthly grant of EUR 5.00 for each training day. Professional vocational development programmes allowing to improve the professional skills and acquire systematic abilities and knowledge suited to the changing labour market demand. After completing the vocational development programme, the unemployed person receives a professional development certificate.

VIII. Measures for the Unemployed with Addiction Problems

69. The measure aims to facilitate the social integration of the unemployed and improve their ability to find suitable jobs, thus minimizing risks of social exclusion. Unemployed persons diagnosed with (or suspected to have) alcohol, narcotic or psychotropic drug addiction. Support measures: Minnesota twelve-step programme, which requires the unemployed person to communicate and actively take part in the support measure. Emotional stress therapy (coding), which involves consultations of a narcology's, psychotherapy, suggestion therapy and drug therapy. Formal diagnosis by a narcology's for persons who are suspected of having addiction problems. The unemployed are provided with transportation service to health care institution and back.

IX. Public Works Programme

70. The aim of the measure is the activation of disadvantaged unemployed by maintaining and developing their work-related skills, simultaneously establishing a better linkage of labour market measures with social assistance services in order to avoid shrinkage of the economic potential (i.e., avoiding that people rely on subsistence farming and/or social assistance). The measure targets exclusively the long-term unemployed who have been registered with the SEA as unemployed for longer than six months. Besides, in order to be eligible for participation in the activity, the unemployed shall not receive unemployment benefits or old-age pensions. Workplaces are created in municipalities (and their institutions and agencies, except state and municipal enterprises), non-governmental organizations. The jobs are non-commercial activities in areas that are additional to tasks currently carried out by municipalities. The period of participation in the activity by the long-term unemployed does not exceed four months per year. Participants can have two days per month off to actively search for a job under the guidance of the SEA or individually having an obligation to inform the SEA on results of the job-search. The two days can also be used for participation in the SEA competitiveness measures, individual counselling, group sessions on job search methods and basic skills needed on the labour market. Compensation is paid to participants of EUR 200 per month. Besides, social insurance contributions are made to cover the pension insurance and participants are insured against accidents at work.

X. Practical Training with the Employer

71. The measure aims to train an employee required by the employer by organizing practical training with the employer. Practical training target audience: unemployed persons registered with SEA that have expressed the wish to participate in practical training and comply with the following conditions: not involved in other measure organized by the SEA; has not been employed by the particular employer at least twelve months before participating in the practical training; has completed the previous Practical training (including practical training in priority industries) at least two years ago, however, in case when the Practical training was interrupted by reasons not dependent on the unemployed person and thus only lasted less than half of the planned participation time, this restriction does not apply; during the previous Practical training (including practical training in priority industries) has not acquired the same competence as on this Practical training; suits the qualification specified by employer. SEA provides *de minimis* support for the employer carrying out the practical training: subsidy for unemployed person's salary for full-time work proportionally to days they have worked in a month (EUR 200 for the first three months; EUR 150 for the last three months); subsidy covering state social insurance costs for the subsidized part of salary; subsidy for salary of the work manager training the unemployed covering 50% of salary for each such person; coverage of costs of medical examinations that are required by law for carrying out the job; one-time subsidy for individual protective gear if required by law for carrying out the job (of no more than EUR 100); one-time subsidy for adapting the workspace for an unemployed person with disability (of no more than EUR 711 for a workspace).

XI. Support for Youth Volunteer Work at NGO

72. It is an opportunity for associations and foundations to attract young, energetic and forward-looking people to their work, and for young people to gain work experience and skills through IT and project management, administrative, cultural and sporting events, youth and other work responsibilities. Besides, the staff of the SEA branches will assist in the selection of the most suitable candidates for the specific activity and requirements of the particular association or foundation from the registered SEA unemployed persons aged 18–29. Any association or foundation registered in Latvia, except political parties, can apply for participation in this NVA event. Participants in the association or foundation will have to work five days a week: a minimum of 4 hours and a maximum of 8 hours per day. Duration of engagement – 2 to 6 months. The young person will receive a scholarship from the SEA – EUR 5 per day, the amount of the scholarship per month will be calculated according to the number of days worked. The SEA will insure participant against accidents, as well as pay for the health examination if it is provided for in the legislation on mandatory health examinations. If an unemployed person with disability is involved in the work of the community, he or she must, if necessary, establish a place of residence or adapt it functionally to the working environment, ensuring free access and movement.

XII. Measures Supporting Regional Mobility of Employees

73. The support (up to EUR 600) lasts for the first four months of employment, helping to cover expenses for transport and/or housing for people taking up permanent jobs with less than average pay and within a distance of at least 15 km from their place of residence.

Chapter 5. Sources of Labour Law

§1. Constitution

74. The *Satversme* enshrines the principle of non-discrimination at the constitutional level in Article 91[125] providing that 'All persons in Latvia should be equal before the law and the courts. Human rights should be observed without discrimination of any kind.' The Constitution generally is regarded as directly applicable. The Constitutional Court has pointed out in the *Compensation of losses* case[126] that the Constitutional norms can be applied directly. For example, while the petitioner argued discrimination because the law challenged failed to provide for the compensation of losses in his case, the Constitutional Court held that Article 92 of the Constitution could be applied directly and that the absence of a specific law could not serve as the ground for refusal of the court to accept the claim.[127]

75. Article 91 refers to 'discrimination of any kind' without specifying the grounds and thus covering all possible grounds. As the Constitution stands highest in the hierarchy of norms, this permit to argue that non-exhaustive list of grounds in fact applies also in cases of laws that only contain exhaustive list of grounds in their non-discrimination clauses. From the human rights law point of view the state is responsible for providing the necessary protection against discrimination in private sphere; this is still insufficient given that the aim of non-discrimination guarantee is to ensure non-discrimination.

§2. Acts of the Legislature and the Executive

76. Legislative power is vested both the government and parliament. The *Satversme*, the State Administration Structure Law, the Structure of Cabinet Law, the Rules of Procedure of the *Saeima* and the Rules of Procedure of the Cabinet of Ministers regulate the procedural issues.[128] Article 79 of the Rules of Procedure of the *Saeima*[129] states provisions on submitting draft laws – legislative initiatives must be drawn up in the form of draft laws and draft laws may be submitted to the *Saeima* by:

- the President (is entitled to submit legislative initiatives, which do not have to be in the form of draft laws);
- the Cabinet (obliged to prepare an explanatory note to the draft law and should submit the text of the draft law and of the explanatory note in electronic form);

125. http://www.satv.tiesa.gov.lv, last visited 15 Dec. 2019.
126. The 5 Dec. 2001 decision in the case no. 2001-07-0103; all decisions of the Latvian Constitutional court are available at the webpage of the Court, http://www.satv.tiesa.gov.lv.
127. http://www.satv.tiesa.gov.lv/?lang=1&mid=19, last visited 15 Dec. 2019.
128. Regulation no. 300 of 7 Apr. 2009, The Rules of Procedure of the Cabinet of Ministers, http://www.mk.gov.lv/en/mk/darbibu-reglamentejosie-dokumenti/kartibas-rullis/, last visited 15 Dec. 2019.
129. http://www.saeima.lv, last visited 31 Dec. 2019.

- *Saeima* committees (standing committees are Foreign Affairs Committee, Budget and Finance (Taxation) Committee, Legal Affairs Committee, Human Rights and Public Affairs Committee; Education, Culture and Science Committee; Defence, Internal Affairs and Corruption Prevention Committee; Public Administration and Local Government Committee; Economic, Agricultural, Environmental and Regional Policy Committee; Social and Employment Matters Committee; Mandate, Ethics and Submissions Committee; Government Review Committee; Public Expenditure and Audit Committee; Sustainable Development Committee; National Security Committee; Citizenship, Migration and Social Cohesion Committee; European Affairs Committee, Administrative-Territorial Reform Committee);
- at least five Members;
- one-tenth of the electorate (Article 65 of the Constitution).[130]

77. The *Saeima* reviews each draft law in three readings. Exceptions are the annual state budget and urgent draft laws that are reviewed in two readings. In the first reading, members of *Saeima* discuss and decide on the general principles of the law. Then the designated committee that is in charge of the law compiles proposals submitted by particular members or factions, other committees, the President of State, the President of Ministers or ministers. During the second reading, the *Saeima* reviews the law article by article. Therefore, only debates regarding the contents of particular sections are allowed. Before the third reading, the committee in charge compiles proposals received after the second reading. During the third reading, the *Saeima* reviews only those articles for which proposals have been submitted. Finally, the parliament votes on the law in its entirety. If the law is rejected, it proceeds to the committee to be prepared for repeated third reading. If the law is adopted, it is sent to the President of State to be promulgated (Figure 2).

The President of State must postpone the publication of law for two months if at least one-third of the *Saeima* members so request. Such a law is to be submitted for a popular vote if no less than one-tenth of voters' request so by signing a respective petition. If such a petition is not submitted during the mentioned two months period, the law is to be published. However, the popular vote does not take place if there is a repeated vote in the Parliament and no less than three-quarters of all members support the law.

130. Law on National Referendums, Initiation of Laws and European Citizens' Initiative; https://www.cvk.lv/pub/public/28862.html; last visited 15 Dec. 2019.

Figure 2 Procedure for Adopting Laws

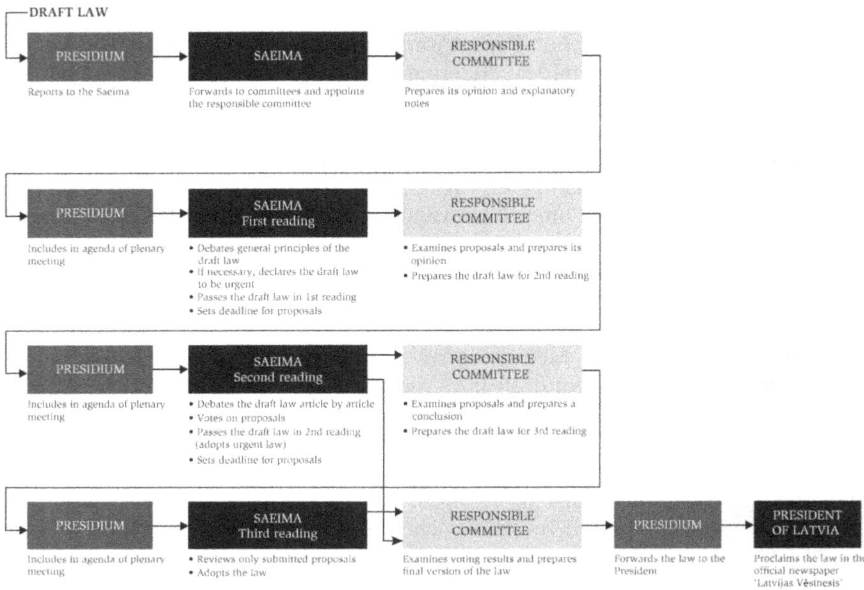

Source: https://www.saeima.lv/en/legislative-process/procedure-for-adopting-laws.

78. The Law on Official Publications and Legal Information stipulates that official publications are published in *Latvijas Vēstnesis*, website http://www.vestnesis.lv.[131] The information system of official publications is a state information system, in which the systematization of official publications and the information included is ensured. The state of Latvia is the owner of the information system of official publications. The Ministry of Justice is the manager and state agency *Latvijas Vēstnesis* – the keeper of the information system of official publications. The state agency *Latvijas Vēstnesis* ensures the systematization of legal acts on the website www.likumi.lv. The Cabinet shall determine the minimum requirements and procedures for systematization of legal acts. However, systematized legal acts are not binding. If a contradiction is detected between the systematized legal act and the official publication of legal act, the official publication should be considered.

79. The Cabinet of Ministers, within the scope of its competence, considers policy planning documents, external and internal legal acts, and orders of the Cabinet of Ministers, informative statements, national positions and official opinions of the state. Upon approval by the Cabinet of Ministers, all legal acts are published by

131. http://www.likumi.lv, last visited 31 Dec. 2019.

the official publisher *Latvijas Vēstnesis*. The Cabinet of Ministers may issue legislative enactments – regulations only in the following cases, including a reference to the law pursuant to which they have been issued:

- when such a right specially stipulated or delegated to the Cabinet by the respective law;
- if the particular matter has not been regulated by law;
- if a law or regulations grant special authority to the Cabinet of Ministers or an individual minister;
- if the particular matter has not been regulated by law or regulations.

The regulations may not be contrary to the Constitution or laws. The Cabinet of Ministers and an individual minister may issue instructions binding on institutions, which are under their subordination:

The Prime Minister, Deputy Prime Ministers and ministers are entitled to issue orders in cases provided for in laws and Cabinet regulations. An order is an individual administrative act that applies to specific state institutions and officials.

In the absence of the Prime Minister or if he or she is otherwise prevented from fulfilling his or her office, his or her duties should be performed by that member of the Cabinet appointed by the Prime Minister as acting in his or her place. This should be reported to the President and to the Chairperson of the *Saeima*.

In the absence of the Deputy Prime Minister or a minister, or if he or she is otherwise prevented from fulfilling his or her office, his or her duties should be performed by that member of the Cabinet appointed by the Prime Minister as to act in his or her place.

The Cabinet of Ministers should adopt its decision by a majority vote of members present at the Cabinet meeting. More than half of all Cabinet members present at the meeting should constitute a quorum of the Cabinet of Ministers.

Government documents come into force after their publication in the newspaper *Latvijas Vēstnesis*[132] (The Official Gazette). *Latvijas Vēstnesis* continues the traditions of *Valdibas Vēstnesis* (*The Government Herald*), which was the official state gazette from 1919 to 1940.

80. On 11 December 2012, entered into force amendments to the Law 'On the referendum, legislative initiatives and the European Citizens' Initiative', which establish a new procedure by which voters can start collecting signatures to initiate law or amendment to the Constitution.[133] All citizens of Latvia who are eligible to vote in the Saeima elections may participate in national referendums and in legislative initiatives. Costs arising from the preparation and holding of a referendum shall be covered from the state budget. A national referendum shall be held if:

(a) the *Saeima* has amended the first, second, third, fourth, sixth or seventy-seventh Article of the Constitution (*Satversme*);
(b) the President of Latvia has proposed the dissolution of the *Saeima*;

132. http://www.lv.lv, last visited 31 Dec. 2019.
133. *Ibid.*

(c) the President of Latvia has suspended the proclamation of a law for two months, and during this period a petition by not fewer than one-tenth of the electorate has been received to put the suspended law to a national referendum;
(d) the *Saeima* has not adopted without change as to its content a draft law or a draft amendment to the Constitution submitted by not less than one-tenth of the electorate;
(e) membership of Latvia in the European Union must be decided;
(f) substantial changes in the terms regarding the membership of Latvia in the European Union must be decided, and at least one-half of the members of the *Saeima* have requested a national referendum on this matter;
(g) at least one-tenth of the electorate has proposed the dissolution of the *Saeima*.

Not fewer than 10,000 Latvian citizens eligible to vote, upon indicating their full name and personal identity number, shall have the right to submit to the Central Election Commission an elaborated draft law or a draft amendment to the Constitution. Not earlier than twelve months before the submission of the draft law or the draft amendment to the Constitution, each signature must be certified by a sworn notary public or a local government authority that performs notarial functions. The draft law or draft amendments to the Constitution may be submitted within twelve months of the day on which the draft law or amendments to the Constitution were registered with the Central Election Commission. During these twelve months, each elector's signature shall be certified by a certified notary public or by an orphans' court that performs notary activities. The fee for the certification of a signature in connection with a collection of signatures for a draft law or draft amendments to the Constitution at the orphans' court shall be set in accordance with the direct administrative costs of certifying a signature but not higher than a half of the fee for attesting a signature by orphans' court specified in the law.

§3. Work Rules in the Enterprise

81. Article 55 of the Labour Law provides provisions on working procedure regulations.[134] An employer who normally employs not fewer than ten employees at an undertaking adopts working procedure regulations after consultation with representatives of the employees. The working procedure regulations should be adopted not later than within a period of two months from the date the undertaking has commenced its activities. Working procedure regulations if it is not included in the collective labour contract or the employment contract should provide for the following:

(a) beginning and end of working time, breaks in the work, as well as the length of the working week;
(b) organization of working time at the undertaking;
(c) date, place and manner of payment of work remuneration;

134. http://www.vvc.gov.lv, last visited 15 Dec. 2019.

(d) general procedures for granting of leave;
(e) labour protection measures at the undertaking; and
(f) behavioural regulations for employees and other regulations pertaining to the working procedures in the undertaking.

All employees should become acquainted with the accepted working procedure regulations. An employer has a duty to ensure that the text of the working procedure regulations is available to each employee.

§4. Collective Agreements

82. Parties to a collective agreement – the employer and an employee trade union or authorized employee representatives if the employees have not formed a trade union – agrees on the provisions regulating the content of employment legal relationships, in particular the organization of work remuneration and labour protection, establishment and termination of employment legal relationships, raising of qualifications, work procedures, social security of employees and other issues related to employment legal relationships, and should determine mutual rights and duties.

The role of collective agreements is constantly growing as a local source of law in establishing the content of labour legal relations. This may be particularly observed in the Labour Law providing that issues such as organization of work remuneration, labour protection and social security should be included in collective agreements. Therefore, collective agreements may be considered as sources of labour regulation to the extent to which these agreements express a common accord/consensus of both parties and as far as the issues covered by them are delegated by law. However, provisions of collective agreements may not be contrary to those contained in the law.

Arbitration awards, like collective agreements, may be local sources of law in respect of persons involved in a dispute. The Labour Disputes Law[135] provides that collective labour rights dispute parties may agree to settle the dispute in arbitrage. The law also stipulates that if the agreement is not reached in a conciliation committee in respect of a collective interest dispute, it should be settled in accordance with the procedure set out in the collective agreement. If there is no such procedure in the collective agreement, the dispute should be settled by reconciliation method or in arbitrage. The performance of the decision taken in arbitrage should be voluntary. If such decision is not performed each party should have the right to collective action. However, if parties reach a written concurrence on the fulfilment of such decision, it should have a power of collective agreement.

135. http://www.likumi.lv, last visited 31 Dec. 2019.

§5. PAST PRACTICE

83. In addition to acts of the legislature and the executive and provisions of collective agreements the jurisprudence of the Senate of the Supreme Court of Latvia substantially contributes to the interpretation and development of statutory provisions regulating employment relations. The authoritative interpretations of statutory regulations by the Supreme Court are closely monitored and followed in practice. Importantly, in 2004 and 2005 the Supreme Court published an overview of case law on termination or amendments to the employment contracts and in 2005 issues on correct enforcement of Labour Law, in 2010 on practice in individual labour disputes. Although those overviews are of informative nature only, employers, employees, by the courts, take them into consideration and labour disputes resolution bodies in solving employment disputes.[136]

84. Customary law in Latvia could be defined as a rule of conduct that has developed as a result of actual application over a historical time-frame; customary law is applied when developing rights and interpreting provisions of law if the issue in question is not governed by statute or other legislation. Customary law plays a minor role in Latvian labour law.

§6. RELATIONSHIP (HIERARCHICAL ORDER) BETWEEN THE DIFFERENT SOURCES OF LABOUR LAW

85. The Constitution does not directly and fully regulate the hierarchy of legal acts. Latvia belongs to the Roman-German legal system that is characterized by strict laws and rules as sources of law. Therefore, laws and regulations in Latvia are primary sources of law (including the Labour Law) and 'soft law' in general is used only as an auxiliary source for the correct interpretation and application of the primary source. International and EU law norms are applied in accordance with their ranking in the hierarchy of external legislative acts. In case of conflict between a Latvian and international/EU law norm of the same legal force, the international/EU law norm must be applied.

The hierarchical system is derived from rules set in the Constitutional Court Law[137] (adopted on 5 June 1996) and the Administrative Procedure Law,[138] which was adopted on 25 October 2001. The hierarchical system of legal acts in Latvia is the following:

(a) Constitution (*Satversme*)
(b) International agreements approved by Parliament

136. Overview of case law on the application of law when solving disputes related to termination or amendments of employment contract (*Tiesu prakses apkopojums Par likumu piemēroanu, izķķirot strìdus, kas saistìti ar darba lìguma izbeiganu vai grozìšanu*), http://www.lbas.gov.lv, http://www.at.gov.lv, last visited 15 Dec. 2019.
137. http://www.likumi.lv, last visited 31 Dec. 2019.
138. *Ibid.*

(c) Laws
(d) Regulations of the Cabinet of Ministers
(e) Municipal rules (legally binding regulations of local authorities).

Judicial decisions may not be considered as sources of labour regulation in general. Article 82 of the *Satversme* provides *inter alia* that judges should be independent and subject only to law. The judgment is binding solely in the particular case, i.e. other judges are not obliged to follow the judgment in a similar case. Nevertheless, judges may use the reasoning explored in the relevant judgment in order to adjudicate other cases. In practice, case law (particularly that of the Supreme Court) and legal doctrine have been used as a secondary source of law quite frequently.

86. Article 1 of the Labour Law stipulates legal framework for employment legal relationships,[139] i.e. employment legal relationships are regulated by the Constitution of the Republic of Latvia, the norms of international law which are binding on the Republic of Latvia, this Law and other regulatory enactments, as well as by collective agreements and working procedure regulations.

87. Article 89 of the *Satversme* states 'the state should recognize and protect fundamental human rights following this Constitution, laws and international agreements binding upon Latvia'. While this recognizes the binding force of international treaties without giving an express indication as to the place of international treaties in the hierarchy of norms, the Constitutional Court has adopted the doctrine that the norms of the *Satversme* have to be interpreted in the light of the international human rights standards binding on Latvia.[140]

The competence of the Court to review the compatibility of international treaties signed or concluded by Latvia with the Constitution, as well as to review the compatibility of national legal norms with those international treaties concluded by Latvia that do not contradict the Constitution must be noted especially since this also indicates the place of international treaties binding on Latvia in the hierarchy of norms: they are below the Constitution yet above the ordinary laws, and ordinary laws and all subordinate norms must comply with these treaties. Moreover, the practice has also accepted that international treaties can be relied upon and applied directly – to the extent that direct application is possible, and the treaties are self-executing – even in the absence of any implementing legislation.

The European Convention on Human Rights (ECHR) and Fundamental Freedoms stands out as particularly important, as not only the Constitutional Court who is by far a leader in using international legal instruments, but also courts of general jurisdiction are relying on it, or at least refer to it increasingly. It also must be noted that the plaintiffs in the Constitutional Court in past years are increasingly relying not only on the non-discrimination clause of the *Satversme* but also on those of international treaties binding on Latvia – primarily ECHR and European Social Charter – and that the Constitutional Court has in certain cases examined, whether

139. *Ibid.*
140. Case no. 2000-03-01, http://www.satv.tiesa.gov.lv, last visited 15 Dec. 2019.

Article 14 of the ECHR has been violated.[141] The core provisions related to employment and social security law are included in the Treaty on the Functioning of the European Union and in the relevant EU directives and regulations. Latvia has ratified all core conventions of the International Labour Organization (ILO).

141. See, for example, the Constitutional Court judgment in the cases 2000-03-01 and 2001-02-06.

Chapter 6. International Private Labour Law

88. Article 12 of the Labour Law states provisions on international agreements.[142]

If an international agreement, which has been ratified by the *Saeima*, sets out provisions that differ from those contained in this Law, the provisions of the international agreement should be applied.

Article 13 is the law applicable to contracts of employment and employment legal relationships:

(a) An employee and an employer may agree on the law applicable to an employment contract and employment legal relationships. Such choice may not abrogate or restrict the protection of an employee that is determined by prescriptive or prohibitive norms of a law of the state which law would be applicable in conformity with Paragraphs two, three, four or five of this Article.
(b) If an employee and employer have not chosen the applicable law, the laws of Latvia should apply to the employment contract and employment legal relationships in so far as Paragraphs three and four of this Article does not provide otherwise.
(c) If an employee and employer have not chosen the applicable law and the employee in conformity with an employment contract normally performs his or her work in another state, the law of that other state should apply to the employment contract and employment legal relationships.
(d) If an employee and employer have not chosen the applicable law and the employee in conformity with an employment contract does not perform his or her work in one and the same state, the law of the state in which is located the undertaking which hired the employee should be applicable to the employment contract and employment legal relationships.
(e) The provisions of Paragraphs three and four of this Article should not apply if it appears from the circumstances that the employment contract or employment legal relationship is more closely linked with another state. In such case, the law of the other state should apply.
(f) Within the meaning of this article, a law should mean any legal norm.

89. The definition of posting is provided in Article 14 'Posting of an Employee' of the Labour Law:[143]

(a) Within the meaning of this Law, posting of an employee should mean those cases where, in connection with the provision of international services.
(b) The employer, on the basis of a contract, which he or she has entered into with a person for whose benefit the work will be performed, sends an employee to another state.

142. http://www.likumi.lv, last visited 31 Dec. 2019.
143. *Ibid.*

(c) The employer sends an employee to another state to a branch or to an undertaking that is part of the group of companies.
(d) A placement agency as employer sends an employee to a person for whose benefit the work will be performed if the undertaking of such person is located in another state or it performs its operations in another state.
(e) Within the meaning of this article, an employee posted should mean an employee who for a specified period of time performs work in a state other than the state in which he or she normally performs work.
(f) The provisions of this section shall not apply to the ship's crews of merchant fleet undertakings.

90. Article 14 of the Labour Law[144] regulates a posting of an employee, meaning those cases where, in connection with the provision of international services: (1) the employer, on the basis of a contract which it has entered into with a person for whose benefit the work will be performed, posts an employee to another state; (2) the employer posts an employee to a branch or to an undertaking in another state, which is part of the group of companies; (3) a work placement service provider as an employer posts an employee to the recipient of the work placement service for whose benefit and under whose management the work will be performed if the undertaking of such person is located in another state or it performs its operations in another state. A posted employee shall mean an employee who for a specified period performs work in a state other than the state in which he or she normally performs work. The provisions of the Labour Law regarding posting of an employee shall not apply to the ship's crews of merchant fleet undertakings. Article 14.1 provides obligations for employer if an employee has been sent to perform work in Latvia. If an employee has been sent to perform work in Latvia, then, irrespective of the law applicable to the employment contract and employment legal relationships, such posted employee should be ensured the working conditions and employment provisions provided for by Latvian regulatory enactments, as well as by collective agreements which have been recognized as generally binding and which regulate:

(a) maximum working time and minimum rest period;
(b) minimum annual paid leave;
(c) minimum wage rates, as well as supplements for overtime work;
(d) provisions regarding securing a workforce, especially through a work placement agency;
(e) safety and health protection and hygiene at work;
(f) protective measures for persons under 18 years of age, for pregnant women and women during the period following childbirth, as well as the provisions of work and employment of such persons; and
(g) equal treatment of men and women, as well as prohibition of discrimination in any other form.

---

144. Amendments to the Labour Law as of 12 May 2016; http://www.saeima.lv and http://www.lm.gov.lv, last visited 15 Dec. 2019.

An employer who posts an employee to perform work in Latvia has a duty, prior to posting the employee, to inform in writing the SLI regarding such posted employee, indicating:

(a) details of the employer;
(b) name and surname of employee;
(c) intended length of employment and date of commencing work;
(d) location of performing the work (if the performance of work duties is not intended in some certain place, specify that the employee may be employed in different locations);
(e) representative of the employer in Latvia who is authorized to represent the employer in the state institutions of Latvia and in a court;
(f) a person for whose benefit the work will be performed (recipient of a service-user enterprise) and a specification of services provided;
(g) a certification that the posted worker who is third-country national, is legally employed by the employer in the European Union Member State, the European Economic Area State or the Swiss Confederation.

91. An employer who posts an employee to carry out work in Latvia, during the posting period shall ensure safekeeping of concluded employment contracts, payslips, time-sheets and documents which proofs the payment of wages by its representative in Latvia, who is authorized to represent the employer at the state institutions of Latvia and in a court, as well as their presentation to the monitoring and supervisory institutions, and, if required by the supervisory and control authorities, the translation of such documents into the official (Latvian) language.

An employer who posts an employee to carry out work in Latvia, has an obligation to deliver concluded employment contracts, payslips, time-sheets and documents which proofs the payment of wages to the supervisory and monitoring authorities for a period of two years after the period of posting.

An employer who posts an employee to carry out work in Latvia has an obligation to designate a representative of the employer in Latvia who is authorized to represent the employer in the state institutions of Latvia and in a court.

An employer who posts an employee to carry out work in Latvia, shall, if necessary, assign its representative, to whom the parties of the collective agreement may refer in order to launch negotiations regarding the entering into of a collective agreement in accordance with the provisions of the Labour Law.

Article 14^2 of the Labour Law[145] provides obligations for an employer who posts an employee to perform work in another European Union Member State, European Economic Area State or Swiss Confederation. In this case irrespective of the law applicable to the employment contract and employment legal relationships, an employer has a duty to ensure for such posted employee the fulfilment of employment provisions and the working conditions, including the minimum rates of pay, in accordance with the regulatory enactments of the relevant country or collective agreements, which are recognized as generally binding. The concept 'minimum

145. http://www.vdi.gov.lv regarding posting, last visited 15 Dec. 2019.

rates of pay' shall be determined in accordance with the national law of the country to which the employee is posted to carry out work or collective agreements, which are recognized as generally binding.

92. According to the Directive 96/71/EC of the European Parliament and of the Council of 16 December 1996 concerning the posting of workers in the framework of the provision of services the employer who posts employee to carry out work in another country, shall comply with at least the following minimum requirements established by the other country:

(a) maximum work periods and minimum rest periods;
(b) minimum paid annual holidays;
(c) the minimum rates of pay, including overtime rates; this point does not apply to supplementary occupational retirement pension schemes;
(d) the conditions of hiring-out of workers, in particular the supply of workers by temporary employment undertakings;
(e) health, safety and hygiene at work;
(f) protective measures with regard to the terms and conditions of employment of pregnant women or women who have recently given birth, of children and of young people;
(g) equality of treatment between men and women and other provisions on non-discrimination.

An employer who posts an employee to carry out work in another EU Member State, European Economic Area State or Swiss Confederation, shall comply with the national administrative requirements of the country to which the employee is posted, and the requirements of the supervisory and control institutions thereof.

When posting an employee to carry out work in another EU Member State, European Economic Area State or Swiss Confederation, the employer shall apply the respective provisions on travel expenses, including the reimbursement thereof. Subsistence allowance relating to the respective posting shall be considered as a part of the minimum rates of pay, if provided by the country to which the employee has been posted to carry out work. Other remuneration which is related to covering actual expenses is not deemed a part of the minimum salary.

Part I. The Individual Employment Relation

Chapter 1. Definition and Concepts

§1. The Different Categories of Employee

93. Latvian labour law does not provide any distinction between blue-collar and white-collar employees.

94. Latvia has in July 2011 adopted specific regulation regarding the legal status of temporary agency workers.[146] On 2 December 2011, the Parliament adopted amendments to the Law on Support of Unemployed and Jobseekers.[147] Article 17(4) of the Labour Law requires temporary work agencies registered in another EU Member State to notify the Latvian SEA before the commencement of the provision of recruitment services in Latvia and to submit a copy of a document issued by a competent institution in the Member State of origin, verifying the right to provide such services in the Member State of origin. Consequently, a temporary work agency registered in another Member State might not be in possession of such a special licence from the country of origin. If this is the case, the temporary work agency shall register an enterprise under Latvian law, because according to the Cabinet of Ministers Regulation No. 458, Licensing and supervision of merchants – providers of recruitment services, only undertakings registered under Latvian law may apply for a licence from the SEA to acquire the right to provide recruitment services. The national licensing system was established following several cases of fraudulent activities of recruitment undertakings in Latvia. Article 17(7) of the Labour Law provides that an agreement between a temporary work agency and a temporary agency worker which restricts the conclusion of a direct employment contract between a temporary agency worker and a user undertaking is void. Article 17(8) provides that a temporary work agency and a user undertaking may agree on reasonable compensation to a temporary work agency for costs incurred for the assignment, recruitment and training of a temporary agency worker. Article 17(9) of the Labour Law precludes a temporary work agency from charging temporary agency workers and jobseekers any fees for the provision of recruitment services.

Temporary agencies are developing as a means of commercial activity. The activities of temporary agencies are defined by the Commercial Law regulating its commercial activities and Labour Law and supplementing legislation regulating its

146. Amendments in the Labour Law as of 20 Jul. 2011.
147. http://www.nva.gov.lv, last visited 15 Dec. 2019.

operations in the labour market. The Labour Law and other regulatory enactments regulating employment legal relationships are binding on all employers irrespective of their legal status.

§2. The Individual Labour/Employment Contract

I. Different Categories of Labour/Employment Contract

95. The employment contract is the main form of governing legal employment relationships.

A. Definite and Indefinite Period

96. Article 43 of the Labour Law[148] provides that an employment contract must be entered into for an unspecified period. A fixed-term contract is permitted only in exceptional cases listed in the Labour Law (Article 44), such as:

- seasonal work (determined by Cabinet of Ministers Regulation no. 272 of 25 June 2002 Regulation regarding Seasonal Work);[149]
- work in activity areas where an employment contract is normally not entered into for an unspecified period, taking into account the nature of the relevant occupation or the temporary nature of the relevant work (determined by Cabinet of Ministers Regulation no. 353 of 6 August 2002 Regulation regarding Work in Activity Areas where an Employment Contract is Normally not Entered into for an Unspecified Period)[150] e.g. organization of exhibitions and sports events; work in cultural events, project management;
- replacement of an employee who is absent or suspended from work, as well as replacement of an employee whose permanent position has become vacant until the moment a new employee is hired;
- casual work which is normally not performed in the undertaking;
- specified temporary work related to short-term expansion of the scope of work of the undertaking or to an increase in the amount of production;
- emergency work in order to prevent the consequences caused by *force majeure*, an unexpected event or other exceptional circumstances which adversely affect or may affect the normal course of activities in an undertaking;
- temporary paid work intended for an unemployed person or other work related to his or her participation in active employment measures, or work related to the implementation of active employment measures;
- work by a student of an academic or vocational educational establishment related to necessary training in a specific profession or area of studies.

148. http://www.vvc.gov.lv, last visited 15 Dec. 2019.
149. *Ibid.*
150. *Ibid.*

97. The term of an employment contract entered for a specified period cannot exceed five years (including extensions of the term), except for seasonal work for which the term may not exceed ten months (including extensions of the term) within one year. Entering a new contract with the same employer is regarded as an extension of the employment contract.

98. There are limited possibilities to conclude other types of work performance contracts. However, the Labour Law does not regulate other legal forms of regulating work performance. Importantly, for the protection of an employee, the employment contract is understood broadly. Thus, if the dispute as to the form of the agreement arises then if the agreement is characterized by elements of the employment contract (a person for an agreed remuneration performs specific work under the guidance of another person) a contract will be regarded as the employment contract. Under the Labour Law if none of the parties has requested termination of a fixed-term employment contract by its expiry and the employment relationship is in fact continuing, the contract is considered to be extended for an indefinite term (Article 45, part 4 of the Labour Law).[151]

99. According to Article 134 of the Labour Law, an employer and an employee may agree on an employment contract on part-time work that is shorter than the regular daily or weekly working time. Several legislative initiatives have been agreed between social partners and the Latvian government in recent years to contribute to a more flexible regulation of employment relations.

B. Trial (Probationary) Period

100. Article 46 of the Labour Law specifies the probationary period[152] – when entering an employment contract, a probationary period may be specified in order to assess whether an employee is suitable for the performance of the work entrusted to him or her. If an employment contract does not specify a probationary period, it should be regarded as entered without a probationary period. A probationary period should not be applied for persons under 18 years of age. The term of a probationary period may not exceed three months. The said term should not include a period of temporary incapacity and other periods when the employee did not perform work for a justified cause.

101. During a probationary period, both parties can terminate the employment relationship giving prior notice in writing three days before termination. An employer as well as an employee, when giving the notice of termination of a contract of employment during a probationary period, does not have to indicate the cause for such notice (Article 47(1) of the Labour Law). An employee has no protection against unfair dismissal during the probationary period. However, an

151. *Ibid.*
152. *Ibid.*

employee has the right to request appropriate compensation, if an employer has violated the prohibition of differential treatment when terminating the contract of employment during probationary period (Article 48 Violation of the Prohibition of Differential Treatment when Giving Notice of Termination of an Employment Contract during the Probationary Period of the Labour Law):[153] 'If an employer when giving a notice of termination of an employment contract during the probationary period has violated the prohibition of differential treatment, an employee has the right to bring an action to a court within month from the date of receipt of a notice of termination from the employer.'

II. Form and Content (Written or Unwritten, Mandatory Provisions, Etc.)

102. Article 40 of the Labour Law regulates the form of an employment contract[154] – a contract of employment should be entered into in writing. If the written form has not been complied with (both parties have agreed on essential elements of the employment contract – wage and work to be performed), an employee has the right to request that the contract of employment be expressed in writing. The employer may be led liable for failure to comply with the obligation to enter a written contract. In order to afford additional protection to an employee, the Labour Law also provides that where an employee and an employer, or at least one of the parties, has begun to perform the duties contracted for, a contract of employment that does not conform to the written form should have the same legal effect as a contract of employment expressed in writing (Article 41 of the Labour Law). If the employer does not ensure that the employment contract is in writing and the employer or the employee cannot in any other way prove the duration of the existence of employment legal relations, the specified working time and work remuneration, it should be considered that the employee has been employed for three months already and that a normal working time and minimum monthly salary has been specified.

An employment contract should include:

- the given name, surname, personal identification number, place of residence of the employee, and the name, surname (business name), registration number and address of the employer;
- the starting date of employment legal relationships;
- the expected duration of employment legal relationships (if the employment contract has been entered into for a specified period);
- the workplace (the fact that the employee may be employed in various places if the performance of the duties of employment is not provided for at a workplace);
- the trade, profession, specialty of the employee in conformity with the classification of occupations and the general description of the contracted work;
- the amount of work remuneration and time of payment;
- the agreed daily or weekly working time;
- the length of the annual paid leave;

153. *Ibid.*
154. *Ibid.*

– the term for giving notice of termination of the employment contract; and
– the provisions of the collective agreement and working procedure regulations to be applied to employment legal relationships.

In addition to the information mentioned above in an employment contract being entered into by the work placement service provider as the employer and an employee who performs work for the benefit and under the management of the recipient of the work placement service, it should be indicated that the employer is the work placement service provider and also that the employee when performing the work, has the duty to be subject to the order of work and orders specified by the recipient of the work placement service insofar as this is not in contradiction with the orders of the employer.

103. An employment contract should be prepared in duplicate, one copy to be kept by the employee, the other by the employer. An employer has a duty to ensure that an employment contract is entered into in writing and to maintain a record of the contracts of employment entered.

The Cabinet of Ministers should determine the classification of occupations, the basic tasks appropriate to the occupation and the basic qualification requirements, the procedures for the use and updating of the classification of occupations. The classification of occupations does not include the occupations of military and State security institution employees. The Profession Classification of the Republic of Latvia is systematized occupation (trade, profession and specialty) list that is designed to ensure conformity with international labour accounting and comparison.[155] This was created under the International Standard Classification of Occupations (ISCO-08). Professions are classified into groups according to the ILO Code, and for each profession have been set the basic qualification requirements and professional tasks. Classification structure: (a) occupation – skilled occupation/type of occupation – occupation, trade, profession, speciality, for which an employee need certain training, knowledge, experience, skills and abilities (occupations are grouped into nine major groups according to the ILO requirements by codes in ascending order); (b) core groups – professions are classified into subgroups and small groups (they joined professions with a high degree of similarity); (c) small groups – professions are classified in separate groups, which bring together relevant professions for some activity fields; (d) professional qualification essential – minimum education level of theoretical knowledge, skills and level of responsibility to ensure the successful execution of the work (those requirements are shown in the small group of professions and apply to all the groups included in the separate professions); (e) performance of professional tasks – each of the main groups, subgroups, small group and individual occupational main work tasks brief description (if the small group is limited to a single group, then the individual groups of tasks are analogous to the small group tasks and are not repeated); (f) professional standards, grouped into five levels of professional qualifications (theoretical and practical training, which allows for a certain degree of complexity and responsibility to a vacancy).

155. http://www.lm.gov.lv/text/80, last visited 31 Dec. 2019.

104. Because of failure to comply with the written form, prescribed by the Labour Law, an employee has the right to request that the employment contract be expressed in writing. For this purpose, an employee may use any evidence on the existence of employment legal relationships and the content of such relations.

If the employee and the employer, or at least one of the parties, has started to perform the duties contracted for, an employment contract that does not conform to the written form should have the same legal consequences as an employment contract expressed in writing.

105. In case of invalidity of an employment contract (Article 42 of the Labour Law):[156]

(a) An employment contract that is contrary to regulatory enactments should be deemed as null and void only for further time periods, and an employer, if he or she was at fault for the entering into of such contract and it is not possible to enter into an employment contract with an employee in conformity with regulatory enactments, has a duty to pay compensation to the employee to the amount of at least six months average earnings.
(b) In case of doubt, the invalidity of a particular provision included in an employment contract should not affect the validity of the rest of the employment contract.

III. Ability to Conclude an Individual Employment Contract (Minors, Others)

106. Pursuant to Article 37 of the Labour Law, it is prohibited to employ in permanent work a person less than 15 years of age or who until reaching the age of 18 continues to acquire basic education. These persons are children within the meaning of the Labour Law. However, there are several exceptions to this general rule. In exceptional cases children from the age of 13, if one of the parents (guardian) has given written consent, may be employed outside school hours doing 'light work' not harmful to the safety, health, morals and development of the child.

The Cabinet of Ministers determines jobs in which it is permitted to employ children, Regulation No. 109 of 8 January 2002, Regulation Regarding Work in which Employment of Children from the Age of 13 is permitted,[157] e.g. collection of medical plants/herbs, packaging of fruit, vegetables and berries, planting and maintenance of trees, flowers and plants. Another exception relates to the employment of children in cultural, artistic, sporting and advertising activities. The Labour Law stipulates that if one of the parents (a guardian) has given written consent and a permit from the SLI has been received, a child as a performer may be employed in cultural, artistic, sporting and advertising activities if such employment is not harmful to the safety, health, morals and development of the child. In both cases such employment should not interfere with the education of the child.

156. http://www.likumi.lv, last visited 31 Dec. 2019.
157. *Ibid.*

107. Another group of young people – adolescents (persons between the age of 15 and 18 who are not to be considered as children) – is also subject to a special regulation. According to Article 37 of the Labour Law, it is prohibited to employ adolescents in jobs in special conditions, which relate to increased risk to their safety, health, morals, and development. The Cabinet of Ministers determines those jobs in which the employment of adolescents is prohibited and exceptions when employment in such jobs is permitted in connection with occupational training of the adolescent, Regulation No. 206 of 28 May 2006 Regulation regarding Work in which Employment of Adolescents is prohibited and Exceptions when Employment in such Work is Permitted in Connection with Vocational Training of the Adolescent,[158] for instance, work directly related to the processing and preserving of fish and products thereof, except cases when the adolescent has the appropriate specialty and qualification.

108. In order to protect young workers, the Labour Law provides that an employer has a duty, prior to conclusion of a contract of employment, to inform one of the parents (guardian) of the child or adolescent regarding the assessed risk of the working environment and the labour protection measures at the relevant workplace.

Moreover, persons under 18 years of age should be hired only after a prior medical examination and they should, until reaching the age of 18, undergo a mandatory medical examination once a year. Special measures of protection of young workers also include a special working time organization, prohibition to employ in overtime work and night work. Pursuant to Article 115 of the Labour Law,[159] parents (guardians) or the SLI may request in writing the termination of employment legal relationships with a person who is under 18 years of age if such person performs work that jeopardizes his or her safety, health or morals or negatively affects his or her development or education. An employer, upon receiving the request, has a duty within a five-day period to terminate employment legal relationships with the employee and pay him or her compensation – not less than in the amount of one-month average earnings.

158. *Ibid.*
159. *Ibid.*

Chapter 2. Rights and Duties of the Parties During Employment

§1. Duties of the Employee

109. An employee by provisions of the Labour Law[160] has a duty:

(a) to perform work with such care as, in conformity with the nature of the work and requisite competence and suitability of the employee for the performance of such work would be reasonable to expect from him or her;
(b) to treat the property of the employer with due care when performing work;
(c) to ensure that obstacles which adversely affect or may affect the normal course of work in the undertaking are averted or reduced as far as possible, as well as to ensure that threatened or already incurred losses are averted or reduced as far as possible. Exceptions are permitted only in cases when such action is beyond the ability of the employee, or cannot be fairly expected from him or her, or also it is prohibited by the employer;
(d) to notify the employer without delay regarding the obstacles which adversely affect or may affect the normal course of work in the undertaking, and threats of losses or losses already incurred;
(e) to undergo a health examination – an employee, on the basis of a relevant order of the employer, has a duty to undergo a health examination in cases where undergoing of such examination is provided for by regulatory enactments or a collective agreement, or there is cause for suspicion that the employee has become ill with an illness which causes or may cause a threat to his or her or another person's safety or health. The employer should cover expenditures that are associated with the performance of health examinations;
(f) of non-disclosure – not to disclose any information brought to the employee's knowledge, which is a commercial secret of the employer and ensure that mentioned information is not directly or indirectly available to third parties. The employer has a duty to indicate in writing what information is to be regarded as a commercial secret;
(g) duty to perform work in the undertaking, unless the employee and the employer have agreed otherwise.

110. Liability of employees – if an employee does not perform work without justified cause or performs it improperly, or due to other illegal or culpable action has caused losses to the employer, the employee has a duty to compensate the losses caused to the employer. The employee is liable only for the reduction of the present property of the employer, but not for reduction in expected profit. If losses to an employer have been caused with malicious intent of the employee or due to his or her illegal, culpable action not related to performance of the contracted work, the employee is liable for all losses to the employer. An employee whose work is related to an increased risk of losses could be liable only if losses to the employer have been caused as a result of malicious intent or gross negligence. If the employer himself

160. *Ibid.*

or herself – by his or her orders or by failure to ensure appropriate working conditions – is to blame for the losses, then an employee is fully or partially released from civil liability for losses caused to an employer. The extent of civil liability of the employee should be determined depending on the circumstances, especially considering the extent to which the balance of the fault has been that of the employee or of the employer. Depending on the circumstances, a court may reduce the extent of civil liability of an employee in conformity with his or her financial status. In the case of civil liability of several employees (Article 88 of the Labour Law),[161] the liability of each employee is determined in conformity with his or her participation in causing the losses and with the degree of his or her fault. Employees who in an employment contract have undertaken the performance of work as joint debtors are solidarily liable for losses caused to the employer. An employee may, wholly or in part, voluntarily compensate for losses caused to an employer and with the consent of the employer in order to compensate for losses, may transfer an item of equivalent value or repair the damage. The Criminal Law[162] provides for liability for disclosure of a commercial secret (imprisonment up to five years or custodial arrest, or community service, or a fine up to 100 times the minimum monthly wage).

111. For violation of specified working procedures or an employment contract according to Article 90 of the Labour Law, an employer may give written reproof or issue a reprimand in writing to an employee, referring to the circumstances that indicate the committed violation. Prior to expressing a reproof or a reprimand, the employer is obliged to familiarize the employee in writing with the essence of the violation he or she has committed and then request from him or her an explanation in writing regarding the violation committed. A reproof or a reprimand may be issued not later than within a one-month period from the date of detecting the violation, excluding the period of temporary incapacity of the employee as well as the period when the employee is on leave or does not perform work due to other justified cause, but not later than within twelve month from the date the violation was committed. Only one reproof or reprimand may be issued for each violation. If the circumstances referred to in the reproof or the reprimand does not conform to fact, or also the circumstances are not such as to suggest a violation of working procedures or the employment contract, the employee has the right to request that such reproof or reprimand be revoked. If a new reproof or reprimand has not been issued to the employee within a one-year period from the date of issuing a reproof or reprimand to the employee, the employee should be regarded as not having been disciplined.

161. *Ibid.*
162. http://www.likumi.lv, last visited 31 Dec. 2019.

§2. DUTIES OF THE EMPLOYER

112. An employer has a duty to ensure such work organization and working conditions as allow an employee to perform the work specified. Work norms should be determined and amended by an employer after consultation with employee representatives.

An employer has an obligation to notify an employee of the specification of new work norms or of the amendment of existing work norms not later than one month before the coming into effect of new work norms or amended work norms, but on temporary and one-time norms – before the commencement of employment, not longer than for three months.

According to the Labour Protection Law the employer has an obligation to ensure functioning of the labour protection system in the undertaking (evaluation of work environment risks, internal supervision of work environment, establishment of health and safety organizational structures and consultations with employees and their representatives in order to improve health and safety at work).[163]

113. Within the scope of an employment contract, an employer may by means of orders specify the duties, working procedure regulations and behavioural regulations for an employee at the undertaking. An employer does not have the right to ask an employee to perform work not provided for by an employment contract, except in cases set out in Article 57 of the Labour Law:[164]

(a) in order to avert the consequences caused by *force majeure*, an unexpected event or other exceptional circumstances, which adversely affect or may affect the normal course of activities in the undertaking (for a period not exceeding one month within a period of one year);
(b) in case of idle time – for a period not exceeding two months within a period of one year.

114. An employer may use the information regarding the state of health and occupational preparedness of an employee, obtained from an employee in accordance with the provisions of the Labour Law (Article 93), only if the taking of organizational, technological or social measures in the undertaking is required. An employer is responsible for ensuring the availability in the undertaking of the information on employee only to persons who, as part of the tasks given to them by the employer, use such information for relevant organizational, technological or social measures.

163. *Ibid.*
164. *Ibid.*

Chapter 3. Working Time, Annual Vacations, Holidays

115. The Labour Law regulates working time, rest time and their organization. Sources of law containing provisions concerning working time are both statutory enactments (legislative acts and regulations of the Cabinet of Ministers) and local acts (collective agreements, working procedure regulations and contracts of employment).

116. The definition of working time laid down in Article 130(1) of the Labour Law,[165] stipulates that working time is a period from the beginning until the end of work within the scope of which an employee performs work or is at the disposal of an employer, except for breaks in work. This perception of working time is identical to that of actual work performance, excluding any interruptions of work, such as breaks and periods of absence, for which remuneration is not paid. Exceptions to this principle are (a) additional breaks granted to employees who are exposed to a special risk, which should be included as working time (Article 145(6) of the Labour Law)[166] and (b) additional breaks for feeding a child granted to an employee who has a child less than one and a half years of age. In these cases, the worker is entitled to retaining work remuneration for such time; in the case of piecework salary to average earnings (Article 146(4) of the Labour Law).[167] For employees who, on the basis of the order of an employer, concurrently are acquiring an occupation (profession, trade) the time spent on studies and work should be summed and should be regarded as working time (Article 137(2) of the Labour Law).[168]

117. There are several types of working time provided for in the Labour Law:

- regular working time;
- part-time work;
- normal shortened working time;
- aggregated working time.

Starting from mid-2009 to 31 December 2018, the Medical Treatment Law provided (Article 53(1)) extended working time for medical practitioners and emergency ambulance crews' persons.[169] Such extension to the normal working hours of a medical practitioner was applied ('extended regular working time'), which exceeded the normal working hours specified in the Labour Law with the requirement to observe general principles of work safety and health protection.

In order to ensure access to medical treatment, upon the initiative of a medical practitioner or a medical treatment institution, such extension to the normal working hours of a medical practitioner was applied, which not exceeded 60 hours per week and 240 hours per month.

165. *Ibid.*
166. *Ibid.*
167. *Ibid.*
168. *Ibid.*
169. http://www.vm.gov.lv, last visited 31 Dec. 2019.

Changes into the Medical Treatment Law states that from 1 January 2019 until 31 December 2022 transitional arrangements are implemented – at the initiative of a medical practitioner or a medical institution, overtime work by a medical practitioner or on the initiative of a medical practitioner shall not exceed an average of sixteen hours in any seven-day period and shall be calculated over a reference period not exceeding four months.

It is prohibited to punish a medical practitioner or otherwise directly or indirectly cause unfavourable consequences to that if this person does not agree to the application of an extension to the normal working hours. If an extension to the normal working hours is applied to a medical practitioner, then it shall be necessary for a medical treatment institution to receive written consent of the person to the application of the extension to the normal working hours not less than once every four months. A medical treatment institution shall perform the recording of those medical practitioners to whom an extension to the normal working hours has been applied and shall provide the SLI with access to this information.

118. In accordance with Article 131 of the Labour Law,[170] regular daily working time of an employee – the working time within a twenty-four-hour period – may not exceed eight hours. Regular weekly working time may not exceed forty hours. Where, however, daily working time on any weekday is less than the regular daily working time, the regular working time of some other weekday may be extended, but not more than by one hour. In such case provisions of the length of weekly working time should be complied with. Regular working time of employees associated with a special risk may not exceed seven hours a day and thirty-five hours a week if they are engaged in such work for not less than 50% of the regular daily or weekly working time. The Cabinet of Ministers may determine regular shortened working time also for other categories of employees. In 2018, actual working hours in Latvia accordingly to Eurostat data were 40.3 hours per week.[171] Article 140 of the Labour Law provides for 'aggregated working time' – if due to the nature of the work it is not possible to comply with the length of the regular daily or weekly working time determined for the relevant employee, the employer, after consultation with the representatives of employees, may determine aggregated working time so that the working time in the accounting period does not exceed regular working time determined for the relevant employee. If the aggregated working time is determined for the employee, the employer has a duty to inform the employee in writing thereof, specifying the length of the accounting period, as well as to familiarize the employee with the work schedule in due time. Unless a longer accounting period is provided for by the collective agreement or the employment contract, the aggregated working time accounting period shall be one month. The employee and the employer may agree in the employment contract regarding the length of the accounting period, however, no longer than three months, but in the collective agreement – not longer than twelve months. In any case within the framework of the aggregated working time it is prohibited to employ the employee for more than twenty-four hours in succession and fifty-six hours a week. The work performed by

---

170. http://www.likumi.lv, last visited 31 Dec. 2019.

171. Eurostat, Average number of usual weekly hours of work, 2018.

the employee over the regular working time determined in the accounting period shall be regarded as overtime work. If the aggregated working time has been determined, the employee shall be granted rest time immediately after performance of the work. An aggregated time system is valued as more flexible for both parties but requires accurate working time accounting.

119. A regular working week consists of five days. If due to the nature of work it is not possible to determine a working week of five days, an employer, after consultation with employee representatives, has the right to specify a working week of six days (Article 133(1) of the Labour Law).[172] In such occasions the length of daily working time should not exceed seven hours and work on Saturdays should be ended earlier than on other days. The length of the working day on Saturdays is specified by a collective agreement, working procedure regulations, or by a contract of employment. The length of a weekly rest period within a seven-day period according to the Labour Law shall not be less than forty-two consecutive hours. This provision need not apply if aggregated working time has been agreed. An agreement that the consecutive rest period for an employee over a period of seven days is less than forty-eight hours is void unless otherwise provided by law (e.g., aggregated working time). It is presumed that weekly rest time is on Saturdays and Sundays. The employer must allow an employee a consecutive rest period of no less than twelve hours over a period of twenty-four hours, in a case of aggregated working time an employer has to provide for an employee a rest period of no less than twelve hours over a period of twenty-four hours and a weekly rest period of no less than thirty-five hours over a period of seven days.

120. Individual employees with a written order by an employer may be engaged to work during the week's day of rest in the following cases:

– if such is required by the most urgent public needs;
– in order to prevent the consequences caused by *force majeure*, an unexpected event or other exceptional circumstances which adversely affect or may affect the usual course of activities in the undertaking; and
– for the completion of urgent, unforeseen work within a specified period.

In such occasions an employer has the duty to grant (at the choice of the employee) rest on another day of the week or to pay compensation. However, persons under 18 years of age, pregnant women, women for a period following childbirth up to one year and women who are breastfeeding – during the whole period of breastfeeding – are the categories of persons prohibited to be employed during the week's rest day.

Pursuant to Article 135 of the Labour Law,[173] the length of the working day before holidays should be reduced at least by one hour. As on Saturdays, it is preferable that the length of working time of such days is specified by a collective work

172. *Ibid.*
173. http://www.likumi.lv, last visited 31 Dec. 2019.

agreement, working procedure regulations, or a contract of employment. The regular working time of a night employee should also be reduced by at least one hour unless characteristics of an undertaking do not allow for it.

121. There are three categories of employees provided for in Latvian legislation eligible to regular shortened working time:

- employees exposed to special risk;
- persons under 18 years of age;
- other categories of employees entitled to normal shortened working time determined by regulations of the Cabinet of Ministers.

Regular working time of employees exposed to special risk may not exceed 7 hours a day and thirty-five hours a week provided they are engaged in such work for not less than 50% of the regular daily or weekly working time (Article 131(3) of the Labour Law).[174] Article 132(1) of the Labour Law provides that all persons under 18 years of age enjoy a working week of five days.[175] If they, in addition to work, continue to acquire primary, secondary or an occupational education, the time spent on studies and work is summed and may not exceed seven hours a day and thirty-five hours a week. Moreover, where persons under 18 years of age are employed by several employers, the working time should be summed and should not exceed the time limit specified above.

Persons under 18 years of age are divided into two categories: children (i.e., persons between 13 and 15 years of age or those who until reaching the age of 18 continue to acquire basic education) and adolescents (i.e., persons 15–18 years of age except those who until reaching the age of 18 continue to acquire basic education). Pursuant to Article 132(2) and (3) of the Labour Law, children who have reached the age of 13 may not be employed either for more than two hours a day and more than ten hours a week if the work is performed during the school year or for more than four hours a day and more than twenty hours a week if the work is performed during a period when there are holidays at educational institutions. Adolescents, on the other hand, may not be employed for more than seven hours a day and more than thirty-five hours a week.

122. Article 134(1) of the Labour Law provides for the freedom of the parties to agree on part-time work in the contract of employment. Part-time work is understood as any working time, which is shorter than the regular daily or weekly working time. An employee has the legitimate right to ask for his or her transfer from regular working time to part-time or vice versa and an employer has the duty to satisfy the request, if such a possibility exists in the undertaking. In order to facilitate effective exercise of this right, an employer, pursuant to the request, must provide for information to the employee representatives regarding any possibilities of employing employees part-time in an undertaking. At the same time it has to be noted that employers themselves possess the right to request the transfer of an

174. *Ibid.*
175. *Ibid.*

employee from regular working time to part-time or vice versa (Article 134(4) of the Labour Law).[176] But a refusal by an employee to change over from regular working time to part-time or vice versa may not of itself serve as a basis for a notice of termination of a contract of employment or restriction of the rights of an employee in any other way. An important principle focusing on equal treatment of full-time employees and part-time employees is enshrined in Article 134(2) of the Labour Law stating that the rules, which apply to full-time employees, should apply equally to part-time employees.[177]

123. Overtime in Latvian labour legislation is an exception to the maximum duration of regular working time. Work exceeding the daily working time of 8 hours is considered to be overtime. The limit of allowed overtime hours is laid down in Article 136(5) of the Labour Law stipulating that overtime work may not exceed 8 hours over a period of 7 days during a reference period which cannot exceed 4 months.[178] It is prohibited to employ in overtime work persons who are under 18 years of age.

Overtime work is permitted if the employee and the employer have agreed upon that in writing. A pregnant woman, a woman for a period up to one year after giving birth, and a woman who is breastfeeding for the whole period of breastfeeding may be employed in overtime work if she has given her written consent. However, in certain exceptional circumstances, an employer has the right to employ an employee on overtime without his or her written consent. The exhaustive enumeration of the exceptional circumstances includes (a) the most urgent public need, (b) prevention of consequences caused by *force majeure*, an unexpected event or other exceptional circumstances which have adversely affected or may affect the normal course of work activities in the undertaking, and (c) the completion of urgent, unexpected work within a specified period of time. If the overtime work in the above-mentioned exceptional cases continues for more than six consecutive days, save when repetition of similar work is not expected, the employer must obtain a permit from the State Labour Inspection for further overtime work. If an employer determines one working day, which falls in between a public holiday and week's days of rest, as a holiday and transfers it to Saturday of the same week or of another week within the framework of the same month, in case of transfer of a working day the referred to work shall not be considered as overtime work.

In accordance with Article 68 of the Labour Law, an employee who performs overtime work is entitled to a supplement of not less than 100% of the hourly or daily wage rate specified for him or her, but if piece-work pay has been agreed upon, a supplement of not less than 100% of the piece-work rate for the amount of work done.[179] A collective agreement or a contract of employment may specify a higher supplement for overtime work.

From 2019 new regulation has been introduced regarding overtime work. With the general agreement, which has been entered into in conformity with the Labour

176. *Ibid.*
177. *Ibid.*
178. *Ibid.*
179. *Ibid.*

Law and provides for a substantial increase in the minimum salary or hourly salary rate specified by the State in the sector in the amount of at least 50% above the minimum salary or hourly salary rate specified by the State, the amount of the supplement for overtime work may be determined less than 100% of the hourly or daily wage specified for him or her but not less than in the amount of 50% of the hourly salary rate specified for the employee, moreover where a piecework salary has been agreed upon, a supplement of not less than 50% of the specified piecework rate for the amount of work done. If the State determines the minimum salary or hourly rate in such amount that the amount of the minimum salary or hourly rate specified within the framework of the general agreement in force in the sector no longer complies with the criterion of a substantial increase in the minimum salary or hourly salary rate, and if the supplement for overtime referred to within the framework of the general agreement in question has been determined in a smaller amount than 100% of the hourly or daily wage, amendments shall be made to the relevant general agreement in such a way as to ensure compliance with Article 68(3) of the Labour Law. If the mentioned amendments are not made, the general agreement shall cease to be valid one year after the date of the occurrence of the non-compliance

124. The night work is considered to be any work performed in the period of time from 10 p.m. to 6 a.m. for more than two hours. In respect of children, night work means any work performed for more than two hours in the period of time from 8 pm to 6 am (Article 138(1) of the Labour Law).[180] A night-employee is an employee who normally performs night work either in accordance with a shift schedule, or for at least fifty days in a calendar year. There are several restrictions on the right to work at night. It is prohibited to employ night workers less than 18 years of age, pregnant women, women for a period following childbirth up to one year and women who are breastfeeding. Employees who have a child less than three years of age may be employed at night only with his or her consent.

There is a specific regulation of night work provided for by the Labour Law. Firstly, working time for night employees, apart from those who have been prescribed regular shortened working time, has to be reduced by one hour. However, if there is an urgent need and it is required by the particular characteristics of the undertaking, regular daily working time for a night employee can be 8 hours.

The night employee has the right to undergo a health examination before he or she is employed at night, as well as the right to undergo regular health examinations not less frequently than once every two years, while an employee who has reached the age of 50 years, not less frequently than once a year. Employers are under the obligation to cover expenditures associated with such health examinations.

An employer must transfer a night employee to an appropriate job to be performed during the day if there is a doctor's opinion that the night work negatively affects the employee's health. Fourthly, an employee who performs night work receives a supplement of not less than 50% of the specified hourly or daily wage rate specified for him or her, but if a lump-sum payment has been agreed upon, a supplement of not less than 50% of the piece-work rate for the amount of work

180. *Ibid.*

done, if a collective work agreement or a contract of employment do not specify a higher supplement for night work. The collective agreement or a contract of employment may provide for annual paid supplementary leave granted to a night employee.

125. An employee has the right to a break in work if his or her daily working time exceeds six hours (Article 145 of the Labour Law). In such occasions breaks of at least half an hour should be granted not later than four hours after the start of work. However, an employer can determine the length of break after consultation with employee representatives, and it may also exceed the limit of thirty minutes prescribed by law. Where a break cannot be granted all at once, it is permitted for an employer to divide the break into parts not less than fifteen minutes each. Employees who are exposed to special risks are entitled to an additional break. The length of such breaks must be determined by the employer after consultation with employee representatives and, as an exception, they are included in working time.

126. Article 149 of the Labour Law stipulates that every employee has the right to annual paid leave.[181] Such leave may not be less than four calendar weeks, without holidays. Persons under 18 years of age are entitled to annual paid leave of one full month. In exceptional cases, however, when granting in the current year of the full annual paid leave to an employee may adversely affect the normal course of activities in the undertaking, it is permitted with the written consent of the employee to transfer part of the leave to the subsequent year. In such case, the part of the leave in the current year should not be less than two consecutive calendar weeks. Part of the leave may be transferred only to the subsequent year.

A special protection with regard to paid leave is afforded by Article 149(4) of the Labour Law to persons under 18 years of age, pregnant women, women for a period following childbirth up to one year as well as breastfeeding women during the whole period of breastfeeding, stating that the above-mentioned categories of persons have to take the annual leave in the current year.[182] It is prohibited to compensate annual paid leave with money, except in cases when employment legal relationships are terminated and the employee has not utilized his or her annual paid leave. By agreement of an employee and the employer, annual paid leave in the current year may be granted in parts, nevertheless, one part of the leave in the current year should not be less than two uninterrupted calendar weeks. A part of annual paid leave may be transferred only for one year. Annual paid leave is granted each year at a specified time in accordance with an agreement or a leave schedule, which is drawn up by an employer after consultation with employee representatives. When granting annual paid leave, an employer has a duty as far as possible to take into consideration the wishes of employees. An employee has the right to request the granting of annual paid leave for the first year if he or she has worked for the employer for at least six months without interruption. A woman at her request should be granted annual paid leave before prenatal and maternity leave or immediately after, irrespective of the time the woman has been employed by the relevant

181. *Ibid.*
182. *Ibid.*

employer. Employees under the age of 18 and employees who have a child less than three years of age are in more favourable position and should be granted annual paid leave in summer or at a time at his or her choice. If an employee under the age of 18 years continues to acquire education, annual paid leave should be granted as far as possible to match the holidays at the educational institution. Annual paid leave should be transferred or extended in case of temporary incapacity of an employee.

127. The Law on Public Holiday and Remembrance Days set the following public holidays in Latvia: 1 January (New Year's Day), Good Friday, Easter Sunday and Easter Monday, 1 May (Labour Day), second Sunday of May (Mother's Day), 4 May (Proclamation of Declaration of Independence of the Republic of Latvia), 23 and 24 June (Midsummer Eve and Midsummer Day), 18 November (Proclamation Day of the Republic of Latvia), 24, 25, 26 December (Christmas), 31 December (New Year's Eve). Employees should not be required to work on holidays prescribed by law. If it is necessary to ensure continuity of the work process, it is permitted to require an employee to work on a holiday by granting him or her rest on another day of the week or by paying appropriate compensation (Article 144 of the Labour Law).[183] If the public holiday – 4 May and 18 November – fall on a Saturday or Sunday, the following working day shall be a holiday.

128. A general clause of Article 147 of the Labour Law stipulates that an employee has the right to temporary absence if his or her immediate presence at work is not possible due to *force majeure*, an unexpected event or other exceptional circumstances.[184] The duty of an employee is to inform the employer without delay of such temporary absence. Temporary absence may not serve as a basis for the right of an employer to give notice of termination of a contract of employment. An additional right granted to pregnant women is an obligation of employers to ensure an opportunity for pregnant women to leave the workplace in order to undergo health examination in the prenatal period with the reservation that it is not possible to undergo such examinations outside of working time. A similar regulation applies to a parent of a child until 18 years of age, when a child is undergoing medical examination.

129. An annual paid supplementary leave of three working days is granted to employees having three or more children under the age of 16 years or a child with disability under the age of 18 years and to employees exposed to special risk (Article 151 of the Labour Law). An annual paid supplementary leave of one working day is granted to employees having fewer than three children under the age of 16 years.

A collective agreement or a contract of employment may determine other cases (for instance, night work, shift work, long-term work) where an employee also receives an annual paid supplementary leave.

Additionally, the father of a child is entitled to ten calendar days leave immediately after the birth of the child, but not later than within a two-month period from

183. *Ibid.*
184. *Ibid.*

the birth of the child. If a mother has died in childbirth or within a period up to the forty-second day of the postnatal period, or in accordance with the procedures prescribed by law up to the forty-second day of the postnatal period has refused to take care and bring up the child, the father of the child shall be granted leave for the period up to the seventieth day of the child's life. The leave referred to shall be granted also to another person who actually takes care of the child. If a mother cannot take care of the child up to the forty-second day of the postnatal period due to illness, injury or other health-related reasons, the father or another person who actually takes care of the child shall be granted leave for those days on which the mother herself is not able to take care of the child. For a family, which has adopted a child up to three years of age, one of the adopters shall be granted ten calendar days of leave. A child's father, adopter or another person who in fact cares for the child and who makes use of the leave shall have preserved his or her previous work. If this is not possible, the employer shall ensure the child's father, adopter or another person who in fact cares for the child similar or equivalent work with not less favourable conditions and employment provisions.

130. An employer, at the request of an employee, may grant him or her leave without retention of work remuneration (Article 153 of the Labour Law). There are no restrictions on the amount of such leave if there exists a mutual agreement. An employer, upon the request of an employee to the care and supervision of which before the approval of adoption by a court on the basis of a decision by an Orphan's court has been given a child to be adopted, may grant him or her leave without retention of work remuneration. Such leave shall be granted for the time period as is specified in the decision of the Orphan's court regarding the care and supervision of the child to be adopted. If the Orphan's court takes a decision regarding an extension of the time period for care and supervision, the leave shall be extended up to the time of the coming into effect of the court decision regarding approval of the adoption. Such leave shall be counted in the total length of service, but it shall not be counted towards the annual paid leave.

The previous work of an employee who uses the above-mentioned leave shall be preserved. If this is not possible, the employer shall ensure similar or equivalent work with not less advantageous circumstances and employment provisions.

131. Pursuant to Article 157 of the Labour Law, employees are entitled to study leave provided that the work has not been discontinued, that the studies are undertaken at an educational institution of any type and that such right is provided for in a collective work agreement or a contract of employment.[185] The study leave can be granted either with or without retention of work remuneration. However, if parties to the contract of employment have not agreed the right to study leave, employers are free to deny attending studies. An exception concerns the taking of state examinations. An employee has an obligation to grant study leave for the taking of a state examination or the preparation and defence of a diploma work, which is not less

185. *Ibid.*

than twenty days a year, with or without retaining the work remuneration. If a piecework salary has been specified for the employee, a study leave shall be granted with or without paying out the average earnings.

132. Article 30 of the on Informing Employees of European Community-scale Commercial Companies and European Community-scale Groups of Commercial Companies and Consulting Such Employees stipulates that members of a special negotiating body, members of the European Works Council and representatives of employees who provide information and consultations, when performing such duties, should have the same protection and guarantees as representatives of employees at the national level in the state in which they act.[186] The representatives of employees should be granted leave so that they may attend meetings organized by the central management, as well as meetings organized to enter into the agreement regarding the establishment of a European Works Council or regarding measures which are to be performed in order to establish procedures by which employees are informed and consulted, providing the average remuneration for this period is retained. The parties are entitled to agree on even more favourable conditions for the protection of representatives of employees.

186. *Ibid.*

Chapter 4. Remuneration and Benefits (Minimum Wages; Various Protective Measures)

133. Article 107 of the *Satversme* proclaims the right of every employed person to receive appropriate remuneration for the performed work, which is not less than the minimum wage established by the state.[187] Article 59 of the Labour Law stipulates that work remuneration is the regular pay for work payable to an employee, and which includes a salary and supplements specified by regulatory enactments, the collective agreement or the contract of employment, as well as bonuses and other kinds of payments related to work.[188]

The Labour Law regulates the issue of equal pay for the same work or the work of equal value, minimum wage, organization of work remuneration, supplements as well as other issues related to pay. At the same time, there are several regulations of the Cabinet of Ministers that determine pay issues, e.g. minimum wage within the scope of normal working time, minimum hourly wage rates, work remuneration for specific group of workers.

134. A general principle of equal pay is enshrined in Article 60 of the Labour Law stating that an employer has a duty to specify equal work remuneration for men and women for the same kind of work and work of equal value. Violation of this principle entitles an employee to remuneration in amount equivalent to that paid by the employer for the same kind of work a work of equal value.

135. Special protection within the framework of the Labour Law is afforded to persons less than 18 years of age. Article 63 of the Labour Law envisages that the monthly salary for adolescents employed for a shortened working time should not be less than the minimum monthly salary within the scope of normal working time as specified by the Cabinet of Ministers. Nevertheless, where an adolescent works in addition to pursuing secondary or occupational education, an hourly wage rate specified for the adolescent may not be less than the minimum hourly wage rate specified by the Cabinet for work within the scope of normal working time. Children, however, should be paid for work in conformity with the work performed (Article 63(3) of the Labour Law).[189]

136. Despite several restrictions provided for in the legislation, the most widespread way of fixing wages is individual contracts of employment and collective agreements. The determination of wages at a local level predominates over their fixing by statutory regulations or company agreements. There is a special work remuneration system for employees of institutions financed from the state budget. There are two main systems of organization of work remuneration provided for by the Labour Law: a time salary system and a piecework salary system. The time salary is calculated in conformity with the actual time worked irrespective of the amount

187. http://www.saeima.lv, last visited 31 Dec. 2019.
188. http://www.likumi.lv, last visited 31 Dec. 2019.
189. *Ibid.*

of work done. The piecework salary is calculated in conformity with the amount of work done irrespective of the time within which it was done (Article 62(2) of the Labour Law).[190]

137. Article 107 of the *Satversme* stipulates that every employed person has the right to receive, for work done, commensurate remuneration which should not be less than the minimum wage established by the state.[191] The minimum wage should not be less than the minimum level determined by the state (Article 61 of the Labour Law).[192] At the same time the Labour Law delegates the right to determine minimum monthly salary within the scope of normal working time, as well as minimum hourly wage rates, to the Cabinet of Ministers.

138. Protection of wages is fulfilled through the special guarantee fund established in accordance with the Law on Protection of Employees in Case of Insolvency of the Employer.[193] The main goal of organization of the guarantee fund is the satisfaction of claims of those persons who are recognized as employees and whose employer is declared insolvent. An employee has the right to satisfaction of his or her claim from the resources of the employee claims guarantee fund regardless of whether the employer has made all the payments prescribed by law. Article 69(5) of the Labour Law provides that work remuneration and related mandatory payments of state social insurance should be first level payments made by the employer.[194] Protection of wages is closely connected to the issue of deduction. In order to provide protection to the workers the deductions from the work remuneration are allowed only in cases specified by law. According to the Labour Law, deductions may be made from the work remuneration payable to an employee in certain circumstances defined in Articles 78 to 80. The Insolvency Administration[195] is a state authority under the supervision of the Minister of Justice. It was established in 2002 according to the Law on Public Agencies, the Law on the Protection of Employees in the Event of the Insolvency of their Employer, the Insolvency Law, and other regulations. The goal of the Insolvency Administration is:

(a) to implement the state's policy in the field of insolvency proceedings – debtor's legal protection proceedings, insolvency proceedings of a legal person and insolvency proceedings of a natural person;
(b) to protect employees' interests in the event of their employer's insolvency proceedings;
(c) to protect the state's and public's interests in the field of insolvency proceedings in accordance with current legislation.

The Insolvency Administration performs the following functions:

190. *Ibid.*
191. http://www.satv.tiesa.gov.lv/?lang=2&mid=.doc, last visited 15 Dec. 2019.
192. http://www.likumi.lv, last visited 31 Dec. 2019.
193. *Ibid.*
194. http://www.likumi.lv, last visited 31 Dec. 2019.
195. The Insolvency Administration, http://www.mna.gov.lv, last visited 15 Dec. 2019.

- it recommends administrators to courts;
- it monitors the activities of administrators' during insolvency proceedings;
- it holds and deals with resources and settles employees' claims from the guarantee fund for employees' claims according to the Law on the Protection of Employees in the Event of their Employers Insolvency Proceedings;
- it ensures covering of the costs of insolvency proceedings of a legal person from the deposit in the cases provided by the Insolvency Law;
- it represents the interests of the state in insolvency proceedings.

139. On 12 December 2008 was adopted, and on 1 January 2009, the Law on Remuneration of state and local government institutions' officials and employees in 2009 came into force.[196] This law applied not only to the state and local government institutions but also to the state and local government enterprises. The goal of the Law was to limit the expenditure of state and local government institutions, including state and local government capital companies, for remuneration to officials (employees). On 1 December 2009, the *Saeima* adopted the Law on Remuneration of Officials and Employees of Central and Local Government Institutions which became valid on 1 January 2010. On 1 January 2011 judges and prosecutors were included in the Law on Remuneration of Officials and Employees of Central and Local Government Institutions. As a result, their wages increased considerably. The Law on Remuneration of Officials and Employees of Central and Local Government Institutions starting from 2011 according to amendments to the Law as of 16 June 2011, provided for a possibility to motivate the most competent officials and employees with additional payments for personal contribution and quality of the work up to 20% from monthly salary. Remuneration in public administration is composed of three parts: work pay, social guarantees and vacations. Around 78% of work pay is determined by the content of the post, responsibility and complexity, while 22% by the employee's performance results and professional experience. Based on the content of the post, responsibilities and complexity, all positions in public administration are classified in families and levels,[197] which are outlined in the Job Catalogue of State and Local Government Institutions.[198] Moving towards a competitive monthly salary for qualified professionals, we intend to ensure gradual levelling out of a monthly salary for employees performing similar operations in different institutions, by narrowing the range of salary scale. The Ministry of Finance develops the remuneration policy for employees of the public sector. It maintains and updates the remuneration registration system for officials and employees of state and local government institutions.

196. http://www.fm.gov.lv, last visited 31 Dec. 2019.
197. https://mk.gov.lv/sites/default/files/editor/job_catalogue_of_state_and_local_government_institutions_2.pdf, last visited 15 Dec. 2019.
198. https://mk.gov.lv/en/content/human-resource-development-policy, last visited 15 Dec. 2019.

Chapter 5. Incapacity to Work

140. The Law on Maternity and Sickness Insurance provides for socially insured persons the entitlement to replacement of income in case of temporary incapacity to work – for the first ten days of sickness the sick pay is paid by the employer, starting from eleventh day of the incapacity to work the sickness benefit is granted and paid by the State Social Insurance Agency. For the first ten days of the sickness, the employer shall pay sick pay in the following amount: (a) for the second and third day of the sickness – not less than 75% of average earnings of employee; (b) from the fourth to the tenth day of the sickness – not less than 80% of average earnings of employee. From the eleventh day of sickness, the State Social Insurance Agency shall grant a sickness benefit in the amount of 80% of average contributions salary of an employee. The average contributions salary of an employee is calculated in accordance with the payments made during the last twelve months, ending one quarter (three months) before the quarter, in which the temporary incapacity to work began.[199] The sickness benefit for care of a sick child is granted and paid for the period of incapacity to work from the first to the fourteenth day and from the fifteenth to the twenty-first day, also in the cases when the child receives health care at the hospital.

From 1 January 2020 for children with diagnosed severe illnesses, sickness benefit shall be granted for the care of a child up to the child reaching the age of 18. These are cases when doctors' council of the state limited liability company 'Bērnu klīniskās universitātes slimnīca' has issued an opinion (opinion of doctors' council), stating that constant presence of a parent is necessary due to severe illness, as a result of which the child requires long-term treatment at an in-patient medical treatment institution; child care benefit for a child with disability has been granted for the child. The State Social Insurance Agency (SSIA) receives the opinion of doctors' council electronically, and parents do not have to submit this document when requesting sickness benefit. SSIA also holds information about children with granted benefit. In case of illness of a child aged up to 18 years with diagnosed severe illness, and if the doctor's council has issued an opinion on the necessity of the constant presence of a parent in addition to sick-leave certificate B, SSIA shall grant and pay sickness benefit for a time period: in case of continuous illness of a child – for the time period prescribed by the doctors' council, which cannot exceed a period of three months at a time. In total no more than twenty-six weeks (half-year), counting from the first day of illness of the child; if a child is ill with breaks – no more than for three years in a period of five years. The doctors' council may provide for the necessity of constant presence of a parent no more than for three months at a time. In cases when treatment takes a very long time, and the child requires the presence of a parent, two opinions may be issued for one continuous case of illness. If an opinion of the doctors' council is not issued, then rights to receive sickness benefit for care of an ill child are determined in accordance with general procedure. Namely, the same as in cases when a child aged up to 14 years are taken care of. In case of illness of a child aged up to 18 years for which child

199. http://www.likumi.lv, last visited 31 Dec. 2019.

care benefit for a child with disability has been granted, sickness benefit is granted and paid as follows: in case of continuous illness of a child – no longer than twenty-six weeks (half-year), counting from the first day of illness of the child; if a child is ill with breaks – no more than for three years in a period of five years. Therefore, if the necessity for special care has been determined for a child by the State Medical Commission of Health and Capacity to Work, based on which childcare benefit for a child with disability has been granted, an opinion of doctors' council is not required for granting sickness benefit. In both cases, the conditions for payment of sickness benefit are applicable regardless of whether the child is taken care of by one parent (person) for the entire time of illness, or by several people by turns, as well as regardless of the cause of illness. The benefit must be requested within six months from the first day of the temporary disability.

141. An employer does not have the right to give a notice of termination of a contract of employment during a period of temporary incapacity of an employee (Article 109, Labour Law).[200] However an employer has the right to give a written notice of termination of an employment contract the employee does not perform work due to temporary incapacity for more than six months if the incapacity is uninterrupted, or for one year within three years, if the incapacity repeats with interruptions, excluding a prenatal and maternity leave in such period, as well as a period of incapacity, if the reason of incapacity is an accident at work or occupational disease (Article 101, Labour Law).

200. *Ibid.*

Chapter 6. Job Security

§1. Seniority and Lifetime Employment

142. The Labour Law stipulates that where a collective agreement or the contract of employment does not specify a larger redundancy benefit, when terminating a contract of employment on the basis of circumstances related to the employee's abilities or of economic, organizational, technological measures or measures of a similar nature in the undertaking an employer has a duty to pay a redundancy benefit (severance pay; Article 112 of the Labour Law) to an employee in the following amounts: (a) one month average earnings if the employee has been employed by the relevant employer for less than five years, (b) two months average earnings if the employee has been employed by the relevant employer for five to ten years, (c) three months average earnings if the employee has been employed by the relevant employer for ten to twenty years and (d) four months average earnings if the employee has been employed by the relevant employer for more than twenty years.

143. A concept of lifetime employment is not used in Latvian legislation and practice.

§2. Different Methods of Terminating the Employment Relationship

144. A contract of employment can be terminated either at the initiative of an employer or an employee. A contract of employment may also be terminated by expiry of a fixed-term contract, by mutual consent of employer and employee, or pursuant to the request of a third party. Parents (guardians) or the SLI have the right to request in writing the termination of an employment relationship with a person who is under 18 years of age if such person performs work, which jeopardizes his or her safety, health or morals or negatively affects his or her development or education.

§3. Terms of Notice in the Event of Dismissal

145. Prior notice is required to terminate a contract of employment concluded for an indefinite period as well as a fixed-term contract where an employer intends to terminate such contract before the expiry of the term. An employer, when giving a notice of termination of a contract of employment, should comply with different time periods, depending on the grounds of dismissal. The notice of dismissal will take effect either immediately, or ten days after the notice, or one month after the notice, according to Article 103 and 101 of the Labour Law.[201]

201. *Ibid.*

However, the period for prior notice can be longer if it is provided so in the collective agreement or the contract of employment. In the event of temporary incapacity of an employee the period of such incapacity should not be included in the time limit of a notice of termination, if the employee requests so.

146. An employer must observe special requirements if he or she intends to terminate the contract of employment with workers' representatives. Prior to giving a notice of termination, an employer has a duty to ascertain whether an employee is a member of trade union (Article 101(6) of the Labour Law).[202] An employer is prohibited from giving a notice of termination of a contract of employment to an employee who is a member of a trade union without prior consent of the relevant trade union. Exceptions to this prohibition are the notice during probationary time as well as situations when an employer terminates contract on one of the following grounds: an employee, when performing work, is under the influence of alcohol, narcotic or toxic substances, an employee who previously performed the relevant work has been reinstated at work or the employer – legal person or partnership – is being liquidated (Article 110 of the Labour Law).[203] According to Article 20(4) of the Labour Protection Law for trusties (i.e., workers' representatives in the field of labour protection) an employer, before issuing a notice of termination, must first receive prior consent of the SLI. Moreover, an employer does not have the right to give a notice of termination of a contract of employment during a period of temporary incapacity of an employee, during a period when an employee is on leave or is not performing the work due to other justifiable reasons (Article 109, Labour Law).[204] If such request from a trade union is rejected, the employer may bring a claim in court requesting termination of the employment contract.

147. In all cases when giving a notice of termination, an employer has a duty to notify an employee in writing those circumstances that serve a basis for the notice of termination of the contract of employment. When dismissing an employee, all sums due to the employee from the employer shall be paid on the day of dismissal. If an employee has not performed work on the day of dismissal, all sums due to him or her shall be paid not later than on the next day after the employee has requested a statement of account. If, when dismissing an employee, a dispute has arisen regarding the amount due to the employee, the employer has a duty within that period to pay the sum that is not disputed by the parties. If employment legal relationships have terminated and work remuneration has not been paid in good time due to the fault of the employer, the employer has a duty to compensate for losses caused to the employee (Article 128 of the Labour Law).[205]

202. *Ibid.*
203. *Ibid.*
204. *Ibid.*
205. *Ibid.*

§4. Reasons for Dismissal

148. Pursuant to Article 101 of the Labour Law,[206] an employer has the right to give a written notice of termination of a contract of employment only on the basis of circumstances related to the conduct of the employee, his or her abilities, or of economic, organizational, technological measures or measures of a similar nature in the undertaking only in the following cases:

- an employee has without justified cause significantly violated the contract of employment or the specified working procedures;
- an employee, when performing work, has acted illegally and therefore has lost the trust of the employer;
- an employee, when performing work, has acted contrary to moral principles and such action is incompatible with the continuation of employment legal relationships;
- an employee, when performing work, is under the influence of alcohol, narcotic or toxic substances;
- an employee has grossly violated labour protection regulations and has jeopardized the safety and health of other persons;
- an employee lacks adequate occupational competence for performance of the contracted work;
- an employee is unable to perform the contracted work due to his or her state of health and such state is certified with a doctor's opinion;
- an employee who previously performed the relevant work has been reinstated at work;
- the number of employees is being reduced;
- an employer – legal person or partnership – is being liquidated; or
- an employee does not perform work due to temporary incapacity for more than six months, if the incapacity is uninterrupted, or for one year within three years, if the incapacity repeats with interruptions, excluding a prenatal and maternity leave in such period, as well as a period of incapacity, if the reason of incapacity is an accident at work or occupational disease.

149. Article 101(5) of the Labour Law provides, that on an exceptional basis an employer has the right to bring an action for termination of employment legal relationships in court in cases not referred to above if he or she has good cause. Any condition that does not allow the continuation of employment legal relationships based on considerations of morality and fairness should be regarded as such good cause. The issue whether there is good cause should be settled by the court at its discretion.

150. An employer is prohibited from giving a notice of termination of an employment contract to an employee who is declared to be a person with disability, except in following cases (Article 109 of the Labour Law): (a) the employee has

206. *Ibid.*

without justified cause significantly violated the employment contract or the specified working procedures; (b) the employee, when performing work, has acted illegally and therefore has lost the trust of the employer; (c) the employee, when performing work, has acted contrary to moral principles and such action is incompatible with the continuation of employment legal relationships; (d) the employee, when performing work, is under the influence of alcohol, narcotic or toxic substances; (e) the employee has grossly violated labour protection regulations and has jeopardised the safety and health of other persons; (f) the employee is unable to perform the contracted work due to his or her state of health and such state is certified with a doctor's opinion; (g) the employer – legal person or partnership – is being liquidated; (h) during the probationary period – in writing three-days prior to termination during probationary period.

§5. Reinstatement

151. Article 124 of the Labour Law sets provisions for invalidation of a notice of termination by an employer and reinstatement of an employee. In case, if a notice of termination by an employer has no legal basis or the procedures prescribed for termination of an employment contract have been violated, such notice in accordance with a court judgment shall be declared invalid. An employee who has been dismissed from work on the basis of a notice of termination by an employer which notice has been declared invalid or also as otherwise violating the rights of the employee to continue employment legal relationships, shall in accordance with a court judgment be reinstated in his or her previous work. The employer has a duty to prove (burden of proof) that a notice of termination of an employment contract has a legal basis and complies with the specified procedure for termination of an employment contract. In other cases when an employee has brought an action in court for the reinstatement in work, the employer has a duty to prove that, when dismissing the employee, he or she has not violated the right of the employee to continue employment legal relationships.

152. An employee who has been dismissed illegally and reinstated in his or her previous work has a right to receive compensation for forced absence from work or for performance of work of lower pay, he or she shall in accordance with a court judgment be paid average earnings for the whole period of forced absence from work (Article 126 of the Labour Law).[207] Compensation for the whole period of forced absence from work should also be paid in cases where a court, although there exists a basis for the reinstatement of an employee in his or her previous work, at the request of the employee terminates employment legal relationships by a court judgment. An employee who has been transferred illegally to other lower paid work and afterwards reinstated in his or her previous work shall in accordance with a court judgment be paid the difference in average earnings for the period when he or she performed work at lower pay.

207. *Ibid.*

153. A court at the request of an employee may determine that a court judgment, which provides for the reinstatement of an employee in work and for recovery of average earnings for the whole period of forced absence from work, shall be executed without delay. If an employer has delayed the execution of the judgment the employee shall be paid average earnings for the whole period of delay from the date of proclamation of the judgment until the day of its execution (Article 127 of the Labour Law).[208]

§6. Termination for a Just Cause

154. An employee can also terminate a contract of employment. An employee has a duty to give a notice in writing one month in advance, unless a shorter time limit for the giving of a notice of termination is provided by the contract of employment or the collective agreement. By agreement of an employee and his or her employer, a contract of employment may be terminated also before expiry of the time period for a notice of termination.

These provisions do not apply if the employee has good cause, based on considerations of morality or fairness. If an employee terminates the contract of employment based on such good cause he or she is entitled to severance pay (Article 100(5) of the Labour Law).[209]

§7. Collective Dismissals

155. Article 105 and the following of the Labour Law include provisions regulating collective dismissals.[210] A collective dismissal/redundancy is defined as the following number of terminations of employment relationships during a period of thirty days:

- at least 5 dismissed employees in companies normally employing more than 20 but fewer than 50 employees;
- 10 dismissed employees in companies employing more than 50 but fewer than 100 employees;
- at least 10% of the employees in companies employing at least 100 but fewer than 300 employees;
- at least 30 employees in companies normally employing 300 employees and more in the undertaking.

In calculating the number of employees to be made redundant, such employment legal relation termination cases shall also be taken into account as which the employer has not given notice of termination of the employment contract, but the

208. *Ibid.*
209. *Ibid.*
210. *Ibid.*

employment legal relations have been terminated on other grounds, which are not related with the conduct or abilities of the employee and which have been facilitated by the employer.

An employer is required to begin consultations with employee representatives in good time before serving notices of dismissal. These consultations are designed to arriving at an agreement on measures to avoid or to reduce adverse consequences of collective dismissals and to mitigate their social impact. An employer may commence collective redundancy not earlier than thirty days after the submission of a notification to the SEA, unless the employer and the employee representatives have agreed on a later date for commencing the collective redundancy.

In exceptional cases the SEA may extend the time limit to sixty days. The SEA is obliged to notify in writing the employer and employee representatives regarding extension of the time period and the reasons for it two weeks before expiry of the time period mentioned (thirty days).

156. The provisions of the Labour Law regarding collective redundancy has not apply to:

(a) crews of sea-going ships; and
(b) employees employed in state administrative institutions.

§8. Immediate Dismissal

157. Unless the collective agreement or the employment contract specifies a longer time period for a notice of termination, an employer, when giving a notice of termination of an employment contract, could dismiss without delay, if the notice of termination of the employment contract is given in the cases specified in Article 101, Paragraph 1, Clause 2 or 4 of Labour Law, i.e. the employee, when performing work, has acted illegally and therefore has lost the trust of the employer or the employee, when performing work, is under the influence of alcohol, narcotic or toxic substances.

§9. Special Protection for Members of Works Councils, Supervisory Boards

158. Article 15 of the Law on Trade Unions provides that the employer cannot terminate an individual labour agreement with a member of a trade union on his own initiative without prior consent of the trade union, excluding occasions where work discipline or the labour agreement has been violated.

159. Article 110, Notice of Termination of an Employment Contract to Members of an Employee Trade Union, of the Labour Law[211] provides that:

211. *Ibid.*

(a) An employer is prohibited from giving a notice of termination of an employment contract to an employee – member of a trade union – without prior consent of the relevant trade union if the employee has been a member of the trade union for more than six months, except in cases set out in Article 47, paragraph one and Article 101, paragraph one, Clauses 4, 8 and 10 of the Labour Law.
(b) If it is intended to give a notice of termination of an employment contract in the case referred to in Section 101, paragraph one, Clauses 7 and 11 of this Law, the employer shall inform the trade union in advance and shall consult it.
(c) The employee trade union has a duty to inform the employer of its decision in good time, but not later than within a period of seven working days from the receipt of a request from the employer. If the employee trade union does not inform the employer of its decision it should be deemed that the employee trade union consents to the employer notice of termination.
(d) An employer may give a notice of termination of an employment contract not later than within one-month from the date of receipt of the consent of the employee trade union.
(e) If the employee trade union does not agree with the notice of termination of an employment contract, the employer may, within one-month from the date of receipt of the reply, bring an action in court for termination of the employment contract.

Regarding the termination of an employment agreement with a trade union member changes in the Labour Law were adopted in 2018 and this constant issue of discussions between trade unions and employers' organizations has been modified. A consensus has finally been reached. Before those changes, to dismiss a trade union member, an employer had to go to court because often the trade unions did not agree with dismissing their members. The condition has been introduced that an employer does not require the consent of a trade union to dismiss a trade union member if the employee has been a member of the trade union for less than six months.

Chapter 7. Protection of Certain Categories of Workers, Protection Against Discrimination in Employment

§1. Young Workers, Workers with Disability and Other Groups

160. Young people – adolescents (persons between the age of 15 and 18 who are not to be considered as children) – are subject to a special regulation. According to Article 37 of the Labour Law, it is prohibited to employ adolescents in jobs in special conditions, which are connected with increased risk to their safety, health, morals and development. The Cabinet of Ministers determines those jobs in which the employment of adolescents is prohibited and exceptions when employment in such jobs is permitted in connection with occupational training of the adolescent, Regulation No. 206 of 28 May 2006, Regulation regarding Work in which Employment of Adolescents is prohibited and Exceptions when Employment in such Work is Permitted in Connection with Vocational Training of the Adolescent,[212] for instance, work directly related to the processing and preserving of fish and products thereof, except cases when the adolescent has the appropriate speciality and qualification.

161. In order to protect young workers, the Labour Law provides that an employer has a duty, prior to conclusion of a contract of employment, to inform one of the parents (guardian) of the child or adolescent regarding the assessed risk of the working environment and the labour protection measures at the relevant workplace. Moreover, persons under 18 years of age should be hired only after a prior medical examination and they should, until reaching the age of 18, undergo a mandatory medical examination once a year. Special measures of protection of young workers also include a special working time organization, prohibition to employ in overtime work and night work. Pursuant to Article 115 of the Labour Law,[213] parents (guardians) or the SLI may request in writing the termination of employment legal relationships with a person who is under 18 years of age if such person performs work that jeopardizes his or her safety, health or morals or negatively affects his or her development or education. An employer, upon receiving the request, has a duty within a five-day period to terminate employment legal relationships with the employee and pay him or her compensation of not less than the amount of one month's average earnings. A person under 18 years of age may be sent on official travel or a work trip if one of the parents (guardian) has given his or her written consent.

162. Latvian legislation provides for a special protection afforded to women employees during pregnancy and after childbirth. A woman has the right to prenatal leave for fifty-six days prior to the birth of a child and to maternity leave fifty-six days following the birth of a child. The prenatal leave together with maternity leave make 112 calendar days that are granted irrespective of the number of days prenatal leave has been utilized prior to childbirth. In any case, it is prohibited to employ a

212. http://www.likumi.lv, last visited 31 Dec. 2019.
213. *Ibid.*

pregnant woman two weeks prior to the expected birth and a woman two weeks after childbirth. The time of the expected birth and the fact of birth shall be certified by a doctor's opinion. The leave granted in connection with pregnancy and childbirth is not included in annual paid leave. The Labour Law gives a woman the right to supplementary leave of fourteen days added to the prenatal leave in three cases: in case of complications in the pregnancy, childbirth or postnatal period, if two or more children are born, and if the woman has initiated pregnancy-related medical care at a preventive medical institution by the twelfth week of pregnancy and has continued for the whole period of pregnancy.[214] Moreover, a pregnant woman prior or following the birth of a child is entitled to several other benefits. Article 37(7) of the Labour Law stipulates that an employer, after receipt of a doctor's opinion, is prohibited from employing pregnant women and women for a period following childbirth not exceeding one year, but if the woman is breastfeeding – during the whole period of breastfeeding if it is considered that performance of the relevant work poses a threat to the safety and health of the woman or her child.[215] Otherwise, in order to prevent any negative effect on the safety and health of a pregnant woman, an employer, after receipt of a doctor's opinion, has a duty to ensure appropriate working conditions and working time for her. If it is not possible to ensure such working conditions or working time, the pregnant woman should be temporarily transferred to a different, more appropriate job. The amount of work remuneration after making amendments to the contract of employment may not be less than the previous average earnings of the woman. There is also a possibility for a pregnant woman, a woman within a period up to one year after childbirth, a breastfeeding woman and an employee who has either a child less than 14 years of age or a child with disability less than 18 years of age to demand determination of a part-time work (Article 134 of the Labour Law).[216] Articles 136(6) and 138(6) of the Labour Law allows for a pregnant woman, a woman for a period up to one year after giving birth, and a woman who is breastfeeding for the whole period of breastfeeding employment in overtime work or at night if she has given her written consent.[217] These women cannot be sent on a business trip (Article 53(2) of the Labour Law),[218] unless they agree.

163. Persons on maternity leave are granted state social insurance benefit – maternity benefit if these persons are socially insured according to the Law on State Social Insurance.[219] Article 5 of the Law on Maternity and Sickness Insurance stipulates that a maternity benefit is a benefit granted and paid to a woman for the period before and after confinement if a woman does not come to work and in this way loses her earnings.

Article 146 of the Labour Law ensures the right of every employee who has a child less than one and a half years of age to additional breaks of not less than thirty minutes, which are granted not less than every three hours. Breaks for feeding a

214. *Ibid.*
215. *Ibid.*
216. *Ibid.*
217. *Ibid.*
218. *Ibid.*
219. http://www.likumi.lv, last visited 31 Dec. 2019.

child are included as working time, paying the average earnings for such time. There are special provisions introduced in the Labour Law concerning the leave of other persons caring a child. In accordance with Article 155 of the Labour Law, the father of a child is entitled to leave of ten calendar days that is granted within a two-month period from the birth of a child. If a mother has died in childbirth or within a period up to the forty-second day of the postnatal period or up to the forty-second day of the postnatal period has refused to take care and bring up the child, the father of the child or any other person actually taking care of the child is granted leave for the period up to the seventieth day of the child's life. If a mother cannot take care of the child up to the forty-second day of the postnatal period due to illness, injury or other health-related reasons, the father or another person who actually takes care of the child are entitled to leave for those days on which the mother herself is not able to take care of the child. In a family that has adopted a child under two months of age, one of the adopters enjoy a leave of fifty-six calendar days starting from the day of adoption of the child (Article 7 of the Law on Maternity and Sickness Insurance). In a family, which has adopted a child between two months and three years of age, one of the adopters should be granted leave of fourteen calendar days.

164. In accordance with Article 136 of the Labour Law, parental leave is granted to each of the parents.[220] Every employee has an individual right to parental leave in connection with the birth or adoption of a child for a period up to one and a half years until the child reaches the age of eight years. It can be granted as a single period or in parts. Additional security guarantees are the inclusion of the time spent by an employee on parental leave in the total length of service and retention of the previous job. Where this is impossible, the employer has a duty to ensure equivalent or similar work.

165. An employer is prohibited from giving a notice of termination of an employment contract to an employee who is declared to be a person with a disability unless in the specified cases. (Article 109 of the Labour Law).[221] Latvian labour legislation does not impose a positive discrimination obligation on employers regarding the employment of persons with disability. Thus, there is no state-imposed obligation on employers to provide a certain number of vacancies for people with disabilities. Employment legal relationship is based solely on rules of open competition where persons with a disability must compete with other person seeking employment on the labour market. The Law on Support to Unemployed Persons and Job Seekers provide for active labour market measures for unemployed persons with a disability, i.e. work practice and training, business start-ups.[222]

220. *Ibid.*
221. *Ibid.*
222. http://www.lm.gov.lv, last visited 31 Dec. 2019.

§2. Measures to Promote Equal Treatment

166. The principle of non-discrimination and equal treatment in employment relations on the grounds race, skin colour, sex, age, religious, political or other convictions, ethnic or social origin and property status of employees was included in Latvian law already in 1996.[223] In 2002 the principle of equal treatment was extended to cover also grounds of disability and marital status and in 2006 to include sexual orientation. Additionally, the prohibition of discrimination was also extended to include access to employment, in employment relations, promotion, work remuneration, termination of the employment contract and occupational training.

167. Article 9 of the Labour Law provides that it is prohibited to apply sanctions to an employee or to otherwise directly or indirectly cause adverse consequences for him or her because the employee, within the scope of employment legal relationships, exercises his or her rights in a permissible manner, as well as when if he or she informs competent institutions or officials regarding suspicions with respect to the committing of criminal offences or administrative violations in the workplace.

If in the case of a dispute, an employee indicates conditions, which could be a basis for the adverse consequences caused by the employer, the employer has a duty to prove (burden of proof) that the employee has not been punished or adverse consequences have been directly or indirectly caused for him or her because the employee, within the scope of employment legal relationships, exercises his or her rights in a permissible manner (Paragraph 2 of Article 9 of the Labour Law).[224] Differential treatment based on the gender of an employee is prohibited when establishing employment legal relationships, as well as during the period of existence of employment legal relationships, in particular when promoting an employee, determining working conditions, work remuneration or occupational training or raising of qualifications, as well as when giving notice of termination of an employment contract.

According to paragraph 3 of Article 29 of the Labour Law if in case of a dispute an employee indicates conditions which may serve as a basis for his or her direct or indirect discrimination based on gender, the employer has a duty to prove that the differential treatment is based on objective circumstances not related to the gender of the employee, or also that belonging to a particular gender is an objective and substantiated precondition for performance of the relevant work or the relevant employment. Under paragraph 9 of Article 29 of the Labour Law the provisions of this Article insofar as they are not in conflict with the essence of the relevant right, shall also apply to the prohibition of differential treatment based on race, skin colour, age, disability, religious, political or other conviction, national or social origin, property or marital status, sexual orientation or other circumstances of an employee (Article 29 of the Labour Law).[225]

223. Article 1 of the Labour Code of the Republic of Latvia.
224. http://www.likumi.lv, last visited 31 Dec. 2019.
225. *Ibid.*

Chapter 8. Covenants of Non-competition

168. Article 84 of the Labour Law[226] provides for a possibility to conclude a non-competition clause for restrictions on competition after termination of employment relationships in written form only if the agreement referred to conforms to the following features:

- its purpose is to protect the employer against such occupational activity of the employee as may cause competition for the commercial activity of the employer;
- the term for restriction on competition does not exceed two years from the date of termination of employment legal relationships;
- it provides for a duty of the employer to pay the employee adequate monthly compensation for the observance of restriction on competition with respect to the period of restriction on competition.

In accordance with provisions of the Labour Law an employee may accept the obligation that, for a certain period after the termination of his or her employment, which however must not exceed two years, he or she will not be engaged in a field of activity in which the employee was engaged during the period of existence of employment legal relationships. Such activity must then be performed neither for another employer nor as self-employment. A non-competition clause can be agreed upon under circumstances where there is justification for such arrangement, i.e. an agreement regarding restriction on competition should not apply insofar as it, in conformity with the type, extent, place and time of restriction on competition, as well as considering the compensation payable to the employee, is to be regarded as an unfair restriction of further occupational activity of the employee.

169. An employer may withdraw unilaterally in writing from an agreement regarding restriction on competition prior to the termination of employment legal relationships. If an employer gives a notice of termination of an employment contract in the case, if (a) an employee has without justified cause significantly violated the contract of employment or the specified working procedures; (b) an employee, when performing work, has acted illegally and therefore has lost the trust of the employer; (c) an employee, when performing work, has acted contrary to moral principles and such action is incompatible with the continuation of employment legal relationships; (d) an employee, when performing work, is under the influence of alcohol, narcotic or toxic substances; (e) an employee has grossly violated labour protection regulations and has jeopardized the safety and health of other persons (Article 101, Paragraph 1, Clauses 1, 2, 3, 4 or 5 of the Labour Law),[227] the employee will lose his or her right to receive compensation for the observance of restriction on competition. If an employee gives notice of termination of an

226. *Ibid.*
227. *Ibid.*

employment contract in the case of considerations of morality and fairness (Article 100, Paragraph five of the Labour Law),[228] he or she has the right, within a one-month period from the day of termination of the employment contract, to withdraw in writing from the agreement regarding restriction on competition.

228. *Ibid.*

Chapter 9. Inventions by Employees (Intellectual Property Issues)

170. There are no specific provisions regarding inventions by employees or safeguarding the intellectual property rights in the Labour Law. Intellectual property issues are regulated by specific laws in Latvia: the Copyright Law[229] (adopted on 6 April 2000; an author has the economic rights to the work that has been created in the course of his employment unless the economic rights of the author have been transferred to the employer by the employment contract), the Patent Law[230] (adopted on 15 February 2007; the employer has the right to a patent if the invention, in relation to which the patent application has been filed, has been created by the employee, the work duties of which include activity of an inventor and research, designing and construction or preparation of a technological solution. If the duties of the employee do not include those mentioned above but are related to the employer's field of activity, the rights to the patent belong to the inventor) and the Law on Industrial Designs[231] (adopted on 28 October 2004; a designer owns the economic rights to the design that has been created in the performance of a work task unless provided otherwise by the employment contract). In some cases, are used specific agreements to safeguard intellectual property, whether of employee or employer.

229. http://www.likumi.lv, last visited 31 Dec. 2019.
230. *Ibid.*
231. *Ibid.*

Chapter 10. Settlement of Disputes

171. Firstly, labour disputes are tried to be resolved by negotiations between respective employer and employee or between employer and trade union. In general, the tendency for employees 'to go to court' is still rather weak; with exception of termination of employment agreement.

The Labour Disputes Law Act distinguishes between three types of labour disputes:

- Individual rights disputes which occur upon the conclusion, amendment, termination or execution of an employment contract, as well as the application or interpretation of regulations, collective agreements or regulations regarding the labour procedure. Such disputes should be settled by negotiation, by a labour dispute commission, or by a court (Article 9 of the Law).[232]
- Collective rights disputes which occur at the time of conclusion, amendment, termination or execution of a collective agreement, as well as the application or interpretation of statutory regulations, collective agreement or working procedure regulations. Such disputes should be settled by a reconciliation commission, by a court of by arbitration (Article 9 of the Law).[233]
- Collective interest disputes which occur in relation to the collective bargaining process defining new labour conditions or regulations. Such disputes should be settled by a reconciliation commission, mediation or arbitration (Article 13 of the Law).

§1. Grievance Procedures

172. According to Article 13 of the Labour Disputes Law, a collective labour interest dispute is defined as a dispute between the parties that emerges during the process of collective bargaining regarding setting up working conditions or employment regulations.[234]

In accordance with the regulations laid down both in the Strike Law and the Labour Disputes Law, a definite procedure should be followed in order to ultimately reach a positive solution of demands brought forward. The first step taken in case of a collective labour interest dispute is the shaping and submission of demands to the other party. Article 14 of the Labour Disputes Law provides that the demands should be brought to the attention of an employer, a group of employers, an employers' organization or an administrative institution of an industry in written. An employer has the duty to review the submitted demands and to provide an answer within three days. If the answer is not given or is negative, the collective labour interest dispute is forwarded to the conciliation commission.

232. *Ibid.*
233. *Ibid.*
234. *Ibid.*

173. The hearing of a collective labour interest dispute in the conciliation commission as laid down in Article 15 of the Labour Dispute Law is the second intrinsic prerequisite of the strike action. Both parties to the collective interest dispute within three days from the receipt of the negative answer to their demands establish a conciliation commission composed of an equal number of representatives. Parties prepare their statement of disagreement and submit it to the conciliation commission. The latter reviews it and takes a decision within one week. The decision taken by the conciliation commission is binding upon the parties and has the status of a collective agreement.

If the parties fail to reach an agreement in the conciliation commission and there are no ways found for strike-prevention, the collective labour interest dispute has to be settled in accordance with the procedure prescribed by the collective agreement. In the absence of such a procedure, the dispute is either settled by method of reconciliation or arbitration or it is followed by a collective action to defend parties' rights, e.g. a strike or a lock-out.

174. Pursuant to Article 16 of the Labour Dispute Law, reconciliation is a settlement of a collective interest dispute by means of a third person acting as an independent and impartial conciliator. Reconciliation can be approached only by the mutual agreement of the parties. During the process of reconciliation, parties are cannot exercise the right to collective action.

There can be one conciliator or a board of conciliators consisting of at least three persons. Only persons having capacity to act can undertake duties of a conciliator. Conciliators can be either private (persons who have been selected by parties to the dispute themselves and which are not included in the list approved by National Tripartite Cooperation Council) or public (persons included in the above-mentioned list). Public reconciliation is without charge. The conciliator is entrusted with the duty to undertake all the necessary action in order to settle the collective labour dispute and reach an agreement. Such an agreement has the effect of a collective agreement. Intrinsic features of the conciliator are fairness, impartiality and independence.

175. The main source of law governing the settlement of individual labour disputes is the Labour Disputes Law. Article 4 of this law defines an individual labour dispute as a disagreement between an employee or a group of employees and an employer concerning the conclusion, amendment, termination or implementation of the contract of employment or the application or interpretation of statutory enactments, collective agreements or working procedure regulations.

There are three stages in the settlement of individual labour disputes. The first stage is the negotiations within an enterprise between an employee and an employer. However, this is not a compulsory stage and its omission does not affect the parties' right to apply to a labour disputes commission or to the court.

176. Where the individual labour dispute is not settled during the negotiations within the enterprise, the parties to the dispute have the right, upon mutual agreement, to advance the dispute to the labour disputes commission established within the enterprise or chosen by any other means for settling the dispute. Parties are free to stipulate the establishment of a labour disputes commission in collective agreements. Exceptions to this principle are contained in Article 7 of the Labour Disputes Law, pursuant to which the following cases are reviewed exclusively in court: (a) the invalidation of a notice of termination by an employer and the reinstatement of an employee, (b) the application of an employer, in case of refusal by the employee trade union to accept the notice of termination of a contract of employment to the member of an employee trade union, (c) the exacting of undue payments, (d) the violation of the principle of equal treatment, (e) the application of an employer or an employee, where the termination of a contract of employment is claimed by a third party.

When the parties favour the labour disputes commission, they should conclude a written agreement providing for the composition of the commission, its competence, terms and other issues concerning the operation of the commission. The commission consists of equal number of representatives from both parties. Members of the commission should be impartial and may not have any direct or indirect interest in the outcome of a particular case. Moreover, independence of the members of the commission during the exercise of their duties should be guaranteed by the prohibition of any interference or influence on their work.

The labour disputes commission should review the case within ten days running from the submission of the application. The commission is not deterred to review a case and should deliver its decision without the presence of any of the parties. The commission takes the decision by majority voting. The decision taken by the labour disputes commission should be compulsory and must be executed within ten days. Where the decision has not been executed voluntarily, the other party has the right to appeal to the court. The decision enters into force after ten days provided the decision has not been appealed to the court.

§2. Role of the Courts

I. Courts of General Jurisdiction

177. The review of an individual labour dispute by a court, in accordance with the civil procedure is the third and final stage. Each party has the right to plead to court if: (a) the parties have not settled the dispute during the negotiation stage, (b) a party is not satisfied with the decision taken by the labour disputes commission, (c) the decision taken by the labour disputes commission is not enforced, (d) the dispute involves one of the exceptional occasions when the case is heard directly by the court (listed above). The fact that the court is the first instance does not serve a ground for refusal to admit an application. Individual labour disputes may not be reviewed in arbitration.

It has to be noted that during settlement of individual labour disputes, trade unions have a special right to represent the trade union members without special authorization as well as they have the right to bring the case to court on behalf of its members. Labour disputes in the court are reviewed in an expedited procedure.

II. Courts with Special Jurisdiction over Labour Matters

178. The Latvian court system does not provide special labour courts.

§3. Arbitration

179. Arbitration, on the other hand, is another method of settling collective labour disputes by which a third, neutral party is authorized to decide by seeking to reach a fair solution and balancing the economic and other interests of the parties. Arbitration can be employed with the consent of both parties either straight after the conciliation commission has failed and following crack-up during reconciliation. Compared to the reconciliation procedure, arbitration involves a more active approach from the people entrusted with the resolution of a dispute. The Civil Procedure Law regulates the setting up and the proceedings of arbitration.[235] An agreement reached as a result of arbitration, like the one reached as a result of conciliation or reconciliation, has the effect of a collective agreement.

235. http://www.likumi.lv, last visited 31 Dec. 2019.

Part II. Collective Labour Relations

180. In Latvia after regaining independence in 1990, the state has played a very important role in setting the framework for industrial relations and social dialogue. From the one side, the state acts as a legislator by setting up the legal and institutional framework on social issues, including the functioning of industrial relations system and the activities of social partners, from the other side it acts as an employer.

Chapter 1. Trade Union Freedom

§1. Freedom to Establish and Join Unions

181. Article 102 of the *Satversme* provides that everyone has the right to form and join associations, political parties and other public organizations.[236] Article 108 stipulates *inter alia* that the state should protect the freedom of trade unions. The Law on Trade Unions,[237] as accepted in 2014, stipulates that the residents of the Republic of Latvia should have the right to freely form trade unions. Thus, the freedom of association and freedom of forming trade unions at the constitutional level is recognized as one of the fundamental human rights and democratic society values. However, Article 116 of the Constitution provides the possibility to restrict freedom of association in circumstances provided for by law in order to protect the rights of other people, the democratic structure of the State, and public safety, welfare and morals.[238]

182. The Labour Law also provides that employees, as well as employers should have the right to freely unite in organizations and to join them in order to defend their social, economic and occupational rights and interests.[239] Moreover, affiliation of an employee with the above organizations or the desire of an employee to join such organizations may not serve as a basis for refusal to enter into a contract of employment, for termination of a contract of employment or for otherwise restricting the rights of an employee. According to the Law on State Security Offices (Article 20, Paragraph one)[240] it is prohibited for State Security Offices officials and workers to carry out political activities, to organize strikes, demonstrations, and pickets and to take part in such events, to form trade unions and to participate in trade union activities. Article 11 states that State Security Offices are (a) the Constitutional Security Office, (b) the Military Reconnaissance and Security Office, (c) the Security Police. According to the Law on Military Service (Article 15)[241] a soldier is prohibited to carry out political activities, join trade unions, organize strikes and participate in them. In accordance with the Border Guard Law (Article 49)[242] a border guard is prohibited from joining in trade unions, organizing strikes and participating in them.

183. The Law on Trade Unions provides that trade unions in Latvia may be formed based on professional, branch, territorial or other principles. Employers should also be entitled to form trade unions. The most widespread patterns in practice are the branch, undertaking and professional trade unions. The right to join

236. http://www.satv.tiesa.gov.lv/?lang=2&mid=.doc, last visited 15 Dec. 2019.
237. http://www.lbas.lv, last visited 15 Dec. 2019.
238. *Ibid.*
239. http://www.likumi.lv, last visited 31 Dec. 2019.
240. *Ibid.*
241. *Ibid.*
242. *Ibid.*

union includes also that of not joining or withdrawing from a union (so-called negative right). In most cases collection of union dues is regulated by collective agreements. Thus, collection of union dues by check-off is common to Latvia and is a usual practice.

184. Article 3 of the Law on Trade Unions[243] stipulates that a trade union is registered by the Ministry of Justice of the Republic of Latvia if the number of members is at least fifty or not less than one-quarter of the persons working in particular undertaking, institution, organization, profession or branch/industry. The Ministry of Justice reviews the relevant application for the registration of the trade union in a month following the date of receipt of the application and statute of the trade union. Registration of the trade union should be rejected where requirements of the Law on Trade Unions are violated or where activities provided for in the statute are in contradiction with the Latvian legislation in force. Such rejection should be subject to appeal in court.

185. Following the date of registration of the trade union by the Ministry of Justice, the trade union acquires legal personality. The Register of Enterprises is subordinated to the Ministry of Justice of the Republic of Latvia and keeps a register of trade unions and a register of associations and foundations (Article 2(9) and 2(10) of the Law on the Register of Enterprises of the Republic of Latvia).[244] The independence and equality of the rights of trade unions are guaranteed by the Law on Trade Unions according to which trade unions are independent from state authority, state administration institutions and other organizations and are equal in their rights. Article 7(3) of the Law on Employers' Organizations and their Associations stipulates that employers' organizations and their associations must not directly or indirectly restrict the right of workers to unite in trade unions or interfere in their work.[245] Article 110 of the Labour Law provides that the employer cannot terminate an individual labour agreement with a member of a trade union on his own initiative without prior consent of the trade union, excluding occasions where work discipline or the labour agreement has been violated).[246] Where there is no such consent of the relevant trade union, the employer may, within a one-month period from the date of receipt of the reply, bring an action in court for termination of the contract of employment. The Law on Employers' Organizations and their Associations provide for special provisions in respect of the relationships between trade unions and employers' organizations. Hence, Article 7 provides *inter alia* that employers' organizations and their associations are not allowed to influence directly or indirectly the right of employees to join trade unions or to influence their functioning. There is no special procedure for the reimbursement of remedies in case of unfair labour practice.

243. *Ibid.*
244. *Ibid.*
245. *Ibid.*
246. *Ibid.*

Chapter 2. Trade Unions and Employers' Associations

§1. Description

186. Article 108 of *Satversme* includes special protection for trade unions determining that the state should protect the freedom of trade unions.[247] The first paragraph of Article 8 of the Labour Law secures the right to unite in organizations: employees, as well as employers, have the right to freely, without any direct or indirect discrimination, unite in organizations and to join them in order to defend their social, economic and occupational rights and interests.

On 1 November 2014, the new Law on Trade Unions entered into force. It replaced the Law on trade unions (1990). The new law is intended to define trade unions and their association's establishment and operation of the general rules and principles of the trade unions in cooperation with employers, employers' organizations and their associations, state and local government institutions.

The law is designed to streamline and modernize the legal framework of trade union activities and to prevent conflicts with other laws and regulations and ensure compliance with international law. In the development of this Law were closely involved the Latvian Free Trade Union Federation and the Ministry of Justice. The new law generally consists of eighteen articles divided into four sections, as well as transitional provisions are provided.

In the first chapter (General) of the Law are provided eleven articles regarding to governing trade union activities, as well as defining the union concept, regulates the right to establish and join trade unions, provides the same trade union rights to organize, determine the trade union independence and equality, regulates trade unions and associations of establishing criteria. The law clearly defines the so-called freedom of trade unions in a negative sense, namely, that the person has the right not to take a trade union and the right not to become a union member if he does not want it, as well as to accurately determine the procedure for establishing trade unions. The law also distinguishes between enterprise-level trade unions and trade unions, which are set up outside the company, such as industry or profession. For each of them have a minimum number of founders – a company formed by the trade unions cannot be fewer than fifteen or about one-quarter of employees in the company if it does not employ fewer than five employees. On the other hand, outside the company trade union may be set up with no fewer than fifty.

187. It also regulates issues related to the name of the trade union, trade union registration, as well as trade unions and defines the legal status of permanent units. According to the new Law for trade unions considered voluntary association established to represent and defend the workers' economic, social and professional rights and interests. Also, the law provides for the possibility of trade unions to keep up permanent units to obtain legal personality, while establishing that a permanent unit acquires legal personality from the moment they entered in the register of associations and foundations.

---

247. http://www.likumi.lv, last visited 31 Dec. 2019.

The Second Division (Trade Union competence and action) consists of three articles governing trade union rights, including the right to carry out economic activities, and their implementation, as well as authorized officials of trade union rights and obligations. The law stipulates that trade unions in representing and defending the workers 'economic, social and professional interests, has the right to collective bargaining, to be informed and to consult with employers, employers' organizations and their associations, collective bargaining (general), announce strikes, as well as the implementation of other laws and regulations of the rights. The law also explicitly provides for the right of trade unions to participate in the drafting of legal acts and policy planning documents at the project development phase, as well as the right to request and receive from the state and local authorities the necessary information.

At the same time, the law provides that the trade unions representing its statutes authorized body or official. In turn, related to economic activity, the law stipulates that a trade union is entitled to its property maintenance or use of related economic activities as well as economic activities, focused on its objective.

Law in the third chapter (trade union representation in the social dialogue and tripartite cooperation institutions, as well as relations with state and local government institutions), which consists of three articles, regulates issues related to the bilateral social dialogue and tripartite cooperation as well as trade union relations with the public and local government institutions.

The law provides that the trade union representation in the social dialogue with employers, employers' organizations and their associations to be implemented on the basis of an agreement with the trade unions to employers, employers' organizations or their associations. Also, the new law clearly states the trade union relations with the state and municipal institutions. The law clearly regulates trade unions consultations taking place at different levels. The Law at Chapter Four (Liability for violations of the law) provides for liability issues for violations of the law.

Finally, the Transitional provisions provide for an obligation of the Enterprise Register of Trade Unions in the register the information in each time record of associations and foundations register, the statutes and information on the representation of parties submitting. It is also envisaged that a trade union, whose department according to the law on trade unions set the legal personality of the unit are recorded in the register of associations and foundations as a union of independent units, converted to units without legal personality or eliminated. Such union's independent unit to be registered associations and foundations register before 31 December 2017, to ensure compliance with the requirements of this Law. The beforementioned trade union bodies, which according to the law on trade unions was set as a legal personality, continue to have legal personality until the recorded associations and foundations register as a trade union independent unit, converted into units without legal personality or eliminated, but no later than 31 December 2017.

188. Article 2 of the Law on Employers' Organizations and their Associations envisages that an employers' organization is a public organization established by at least five employers, which represents and protects the economic, social and professional interests of its members, as well as other interests that conform to the objectives and functions of the employers' organization.[248] Members of an employers' organization may be natural or legal persons who on the basis of a contract of employment employ at least one employee. Article 2 of the Law on Employers' Organizations and their Associations[249] stipulates that an employers' organization is a public organization founded by at least five employers and which represents and protects economic, social and professional interests of its members.

Trade unions are founded in different sectors, for example, electricity, medicine, security, municipality, transport, police, telecommunications industry. They may be formed on the basis of professional, regional or other principles[250] . According to the statistics of *Lursoft* in the Register of Enterprises of the Republic of Latvia 123 trade union are registered.[251] The Free Trade Union Confederation of Latvia unites twenty different branch trade unions or professional trade union organizations.[252]

§2. Role and Structure

189. The National Tripartite Cooperation Council is composed of an equal number of representatives of participating parties. Each participating party nominates nine representatives, among other things a chairperson of each participating party and its substitute in the Council. The Prime Minister convenes the meeting of Council. In the absence of the Prime Minister, the Minister of Welfare convenes the meeting of Council. The secretary of Council ensures technical activity of the Council. The secretary of the Council institutionally is subordinated to the director of the State Chancellery and functionally – to the Prime Minister. Meeting of the Council is valid with nothing less than seven representatives of each participating party. The institutional system of the NTCC comprises ten sub-councils in accordance with the scope of issues considered by them. Ten sub-councils have been established on the following areas: social security; labour affairs; professional education and employment; health care; environmental protection; regional development; transport, communications and information technologies; public security; budget and taxes; environment protection; competitiveness and sustainability.

190. The main contract establishing the framework of social dialogue at the national level is the tripartite agreement from 1 October 2004, signed by the Free Trade Union Confederation of Latvia, the Employers' Confederation of Latvia and the Government. A decision was made by the two organizations to sign a new General Agreement in early 2007, desiring to continue and extend the successful cooperation to date in the creation of a favourable socio-economic environment and the provision of social peace. The Employers' Confederation of Latvia and Free Trade Union Federation of Latvia (LBAS) agreed to work together at international, European, national, local, sectoral, and company levels to achieve common objectives

248. *Ibid.*
249. *Ibid.*
250. Law on Trade Unions.
251. http://www.ur.gov.lv/?a=1104, last visited 15 Dec. 2019.
252. http://www.lbas.lv, last visited 15 Dec. 2019.

that are aimed at promoting the sustainable development of the Latvian economy; creating favourable social conditions and promoting the welfare of the population; improving the culture of employment relations and the working environment and building a strong organised civil society. In 2013 the Employers' Confederation of Latvia and LBAS renewed the General Agreement. Both organizations agreed to continue to develop cooperation and promote bipartite and tripartite social dialogue in the development of policy planning documents and legislative projects in education, employment, labour law, labour protection, social security, equal opportunities, financial – economic, environmental, transport and social development, and corporate social responsibility areas. The Parties agree that the prerequisite for defining common objectives and interests and on the action up to 2020 is the sustainable development of the Latvian economy ensuring competitive jobs and adequate wages, increasing productivity and efficiency, implementing structural reforms, creating products and services with high added value.

Over the years, social partners' cooperation in the framework of the NTCC has been efficient. The current model of national-level social and economic negotiations between trade unions, employers' organizations and the government is well structured, with already rooted traditions and is an efficient model for Latvia.

Chapter 3. Institutionalized Relations Between Employers and Employees

191. In accordance with Article 10 of the Labour Law, employees should exercise the defence of their social, economic and occupational rights and interests directly, or indirectly through the mediation of employee representatives.[253] Employee representatives should mean:

- an employee trade union on behalf of which a trade union institution or an official authorized by the articles of association of the trade union acts; or
- authorized employee representatives who have been elected in accordance with the law. The most common way of representation is a trade union representation.

Currently, there are no workers' councils or committees in Latvia at national level within the conventional meaning of these establishments. At the same time, the Labour Protection Law provides for a trusted representative institution, which should be established in order to represent the interests of employees regarding labour protection.[254] Thus, if in the undertaking, at least ten trusted representatives are elected; they should establish a trusted representative committee, which should co-ordinate the work of the trusted representatives.

192. However, works councils' regulation within their conventional meaning exists at the European level. The Law on Informing Employees of European Community-scale Commercial Companies and European Community-scale Groups of Commercial Companies and Consulting Such Employees transposes the Directive EEC 94/45 laying down the obligation to establish European Works Council or another information and consultation mechanism in European scale companies and groups of undertakings.[255]

Authorized employee representatives may be elected if an undertaking employs five or more employees. They should express a united view with respect to the employer.

If there are several employee trade unions, they should authorize their representatives for joint negotiations with an employer in proportion to the number of members of each trade union but not less than one representative each.

It is prohibited to apply sanctions to an employee or to otherwise directly or indirectly cause adverse consequences for him or her because the employee, within the scope of employment legal relationships, exercises his or her rights in a permissible manner.

Generally, employee representatives should be elected for a specified term of office, which is set out in the collective agreement. As regards the Labour Protection Law, trusted representatives of workers or their professional organizations that are elected in order to represent the interests of workers within the undertaking with

253. http://www.likumi.lv, last visited 31 Dec. 2019.
254. http://www.likumi.lv, last visited 31 Dec. 2019.
255. *Ibid.*

respect to labour protection should be elected for a term of three years if not specified otherwise in the collective agreement. The Law on Strikes authorizes employee and trade union representatives to establish a conciliation committee in case of a labour interest dispute (pre-strike negotiations). In such event the term of office for the representatives should be the one of the fulfilments of a specific task.

193. Employee representatives, when performing their duties, have the following rights (Article 11 of the Labour Law):[256]

- the right to request and receive from the employer information regarding the economic and social situation of the undertaking;
- the right to receive information in good time and consult with the employer before the employer takes such decisions as may affect the interests of employees, in particular a decision which may substantially affect work remuneration, working conditions and employment in the undertaking;
- the right to take part in the determination and improvement of work remuneration provisions, working environment, working conditions and organization of working time, as well as in protecting the safety and health of employees;
- the right to enter the territory of the undertaking, as well as to have access to workplaces;
- the right to hold meetings of employees in the territory and premises of the undertaking; and
- the right to monitor how regulatory enactments, the collective work agreement and working procedure regulations are being observed in employment legal relationships.

The rights of employee representatives must be exercised so that the efficiency of the operations of the undertaking is not reduced. Employee representatives have the duty not to disclose information brought to their attention that is a commercial secret of the employer. However, such information must be indicated in writing. Performance of the duties of an employee representative may not serve as a basis for refusal to enter a contract of employment, for termination of a contract of employment, or for otherwise restricting the rights of an employee.

194. Currently, co-determination rights are not well developed in Latvia and exist only to the extent that is determined by collective agreements. Work councils do not exist at the national level either. Nevertheless, there is a law regarding European Works Councils (on Informing Employees of European Community-scale Commercial Companies and European Community-scale Groups of Commercial Companies and Consulting such Employees), which is meant to be one of the co-determination mechanisms at the European level.

195. Authorized employee representatives may be elected if an undertaking employs five or more employees. They should express a united view concerning the employer.

---

256. *Ibid.*

If there are several employee trade unions, they should authorize their representatives for joint negotiations with an employer in proportion to the number of members of each trade union but not less than one representative each.

Chapter 4. Collective Bargaining

196. The collective bargaining authority in Latvia mostly is in the hands of employees and employers' organizations themselves. The role of the state is to provide them with the necessary framework decisions in order to make their activities as effective as possible. The general right to collective bargaining stems from the *Satversme* (Article 108) whereby employed persons have the right to a collective labour agreement, and the right to strike.[257] Issues as to collective agreements are enshrined in the Labour Law, while the right to collective action is contained in the Strike Law. Some issues of collective bargaining may also be found in the Labour Disputes Law. The necessary legal background for trade unions and employers' organizations is contained in Law on Trade Unions and the Law on Employers' Organizations and their Associations respectively. For instance, Article 11 of the Law on Employers' Organizations and their Associations promotes and makes it the responsibility of the employers' organizations or their associations to recognize trade unions, involved in negotiations with them, conclude collective labour agreements and general agreements.[258]

197. In Latvia, collective bargaining takes place mainly at two levels: the company level and the branch level. Some Latvian lawyers conclude that the 'main aim of collective agreements is more effectively safeguard the interests of employees, which is not an easy task for each individual employee. It is true that a collective agreement restricts private autonomy in concluding the individual employment agreement, although it protects employees from unilaterally imposed provisions for the sake of employer'.[259] A useful example of cooperation between social partners and the government is a memorandum of understanding, signed on 31 May 2016 by the Prime Minister, the Minister of Economics, the Minister of Finance and twelve construction associations, pledging mutual trust and cooperation in fighting shadow economy. The Memorandum sets out to reduce the shadow economy in construction, which currently accounts for an estimated 40%, by half in three years' time. The Latvian Partnership of Building Contractors commits to funding an annual assessment of the industry's shadow economy and to work out an annual action plan for combating the shadow economy.[260]

§1. Levels of Bargaining

198. Parties to collective bargaining at the company level are the employer, the employee trade union or authorized employee representatives if the employees have not formed a trade union. A collective work agreement in a sector or territory (general agreement) should be entered into by an employer, a group of employers, an organization of employers or an association of organizations of employers, and an

257. http://www.satv.tiesa.gov.lv, last visited 15 Dec. 2019.
258. http://www.likumi.lv, last visited 31 Dec. 2019.
259. Kaspars Balodis, 'Levads civiltiesibàs', Rīga, *Zvaigzne ABC*, 2007, p. 43.
260. http://www.baltic-course.com/eng/real_estate/?doc=121485, last visited 23 Jul. 2016.

employee trade union or an association (union) of employee trade unions if the parties to the general agreement have relevant authorization or if the right to enter into a general agreement is provided for by the Arts of association of such associations (unions).

199. Collective agreements in Latvia cover 14%–16% of employed persons.[261] Latvia is one of the EU Member states with collective agreement coverage of less than 35%. The research carried out within the framework of the project 'Strengthening the Administrative Capacity of the Free Trade Union Confederation of Latvia' shows that in Latvia collective agreement coverage is 24%. From 1 June 2017, a project had been launched to conclude five framework agreements: transport, chemistry and pharmacy, communications, construction.

200. The entering into a collective agreement should be proposed by employee representatives, the employer or their associations (unions). An employer is not entitled to refuse to enter into negotiations regarding the conclusion of a collective work agreement. A reply in writing to a proposal of collective bargaining should be provided within ten days from the date of receipt of the proposal. Parties entering into a collective work agreement should organize negotiations and agree on the procedures for the formulation and discussion of the collective work agreement.

201. If during the course of negotiations, an agreement on the procedures for formulation and discussion of a collective work agreement, or the content of the collective work agreement is not reached due to the objections of one party, such party has a duty, not later than within ten days, to give a reply in writing to the proposals expressed by the other party. If a draft of the whole collective work agreement is received, a reply in writing should be provided not later than within a one-month period and the party should include in it its objections and proposals regarding the draft. Any employee has the right to submit in writing to the parties to a collective work agreement his or her proposals with respect to a draft collective work agreement.

§2. Content of Bargaining

202. Article 17 of the Labour Law stipulates a content and form of collective agreements, that parties to a collective agreement shall reach agreement on the provisions regulating the content of employment legal relationships, in particular the organization of work remuneration and labour protection, establishment and termination of employment legal relationships, raising of qualifications, work procedures, social security of employees and other issues related to employment legal relationships, and shall determine mutual rights and duties.[262]

261. https://arodbiedribas.lv/, last visited 15 Dec. 2019.
262. http://www.likumi.lv, last visited 31 Dec. 2019.

203. A collective work agreement is binding on the parties and its provisions apply to all employees who are employed by the relevant employer, unless provided for otherwise in the collective work agreement. It is of no consequence whether employment legal relationships with the employee were established prior to or after the coming into effect of the collective work agreement. An employee and an employer may derogate from the provisions of a collective work agreement only if the relevant provisions of the contract of employment are more favourable to the employee. A general agreement entered into by an organization of employers or an association of organizations of employers should be binding on the members of the organization or the association of organizations.

§3. Extension and Interpretation

204. If members of an organization of employers or an association of employers' organizations employ more than 50% of the employees in a sector, a general agreement entered into between them and an employee trade union or an association (union) of employee trade unions is binding on all employers of the relevant sector and applies to all employees employed by the employers. With respect to such employers and employees, the general agreement comes into effect on the day of its publication in the newspaper *Latvijas Vēstnesis* (official newspaper of the Republic of Latvia), after a joint application of the parties.

205. A collective work agreement should be entered into for a specified period or for a period of time required for the performance of specific work. A collective work agreement should come into effect on the date it was entered into, unless the collective work agreement specifies another time for coming into effect. If a collective work agreement does not specify a time of effect, the collective work agreement should be deemed to have been entered into for one year.

206. A collective work agreement may be terminated before the expiry of its term based on:

(a) agreement by the parties; or
(b) notice of termination by one party if such right has been agreed upon in the collective work agreement.

Upon termination of a collective work agreement its provisions should apply up to the time of coming into effect of a new collective work agreement, unless agreed otherwise by the parties.

A recent example is a general agreement on minimum wage in the construction sector, which came in force 3 November 2019. It states that the minimum gross wage is to reach EUR 780 from EUR 430 and hourly rate EUR 4.67 in the entire industry in Latvia. Employees have the right to a monthly education benefit of 5% (EUR 39) for any job-relevant training. Employers, on the other hand, are entitled to define six months′ summary working time accounting period and to compensate for overtime at 50% of the wage amount. The agreement also outlines to option to receive 5% bonus if the employed person has the appropriate education, which guarantees a wage of EUR 820. The comprehensive general agreement in the construction sector is an agreement for a considerable increase in minimum wages, which means higher social protection and social guarantees for employees in the construction sector. According to estimates from the Latvian Construction Contractors Partnership, changes will directly affect more than 30,000 persons. The general agreement in the construction sector is generally binding *erga omnes* collective agreement. It is concluded between employers (Latvian Building Contractors, the Latvian Builders 'Association, the Latvian Road Builders, and different companies) and Latvian Builders Trade Union. It has been concluded for the period from 3 November 2019, until 31 December 2025, and covers all the employers and employees within the construction sector.

This agreement provides for a projected wage growth setting the minimum wage at EUR 780 per month and monthly education benefit of 5% (EUR 39) for any job-relevant training. Employers, on the other hand, are entitled to define 6 months' summary working time accounting period and to compensate for overtime at 50% of the wage amount.

Chapter 5. Strikes, Lock-Outs and Other Legal Forms of Industrial Action

§1. Regulation

207. The employees' right to strike is one of the fundamental rights in Latvia and is secured in Article 108 of the *Satversme*.[263] The main legislative acts dealing with strike issues are the Strike Law,[264] determining rights and duties of all parties involved, restrictions to striking rights, the procedure of strike monitoring, responsibility for violation of the right to strike, etc., as well as the Labour Dispute Law.[265] There are several other legislative acts laying down restrictions to the right to strike on specific categories of employees. According to Article 1(3) of the Strike Law, a strike is a last resort means of settling a collective labour interest dispute when employees voluntarily wholly or partly terminate their work in order to reach the implementation of their demands.[266] According to Article 4 of the Strike Law, an employee can neither be forced to participate nor restrained from participating in a strike.[267]

208. According to the Satversme and Article 3 of the Strike Law, employees are entitled the right to strike in order to protect their economic or professional interests. This general right, however, is not absolute and can be restricted in public interest in respect of certain categories of persons, including judges, public prosecutors, police officers, firefighters, border-guards, employees of state security institutions, warders of imprisonment and persons serving in National Armed Forces, who are not allowed to strike as foreseen in Article 16 of Strike Law.[268] Furthermore, pursuant to Article 13(1.4) of the Law On State of Emergency,[269] the Cabinet of Ministers has a right while declaring the state of emergency, to prohibit any strikes for a certain period of time. The announcement or participation in a strike is not considered as a violation of the Labour Law or a contract of employment. It, therefore, cannot serve as the ground for dismissal of an employee (Article 26(1) of the Strike Law).[270] Employees participating in a strike in conformity with the procedure laid down in the Strike Law and the Labour Disputes Law retain their office and are not subject to disciplinary punishment.

209. Employees participating in a strike do not receive regular pay for work and social insurance payments for this period unless otherwise agreed in a collective agreement. Nevertheless, those employees working in essential services during the strike receive regular pay for work in accordance with the work done. Other employees not participating in the strike and continuing their work receive regular

263. http://www.satv.tiesa.gov.lv/?lang=2&mid=.doc, last visited 15 Dec. 2019.
264. http://www.likumi.lv, last visited 31 Dec. 2019.
265. *Ibid.*
266. *Ibid.*
267. *Ibid.*
268. *Ibid.*
269. *Ibid.*
270. http://www.likumi.lv, last visited 31 Dec. 2019.

pay for work in accordance with their employment contract and collective agreement and remain bound by them. The latter cannot be forced to undertake the work of employees participating in a strike.

210. Trade unions, the employee's authorized representatives or employees themselves have the right to announce a strike on four occasions:

(1) the right can be exercised if the collective labour interest dispute has not been settled in a conciliation commission and the parties have not agreed on settling the dispute by a method of reconciliation or by arbitration;
(2) such a right applies when the parties fail to settle the dispute by reconciliation, and the parties do not resort to arbitration;
(3) a party has the right to strike when, within ten days, procedural requirements such as the establishment of a conciliation commission or the commencement of the resolution of a dispute before a commission, reconciliation or arbitration are not observed;
(4) the strike can be launched if the employer (or employer's organization) violates an agreement reached during any stage of negotiations. In the latter occasion, the strict procedure of initiation of a strike can be ignored.

211. According to Article 13 of the Strike Law, a trade union, upon a decision of the strike announcement, should establish a strike committee that would lead the strike and would represent interests of relevant trade unions or employees of an enterprise during strike negotiations with an employer.[271] No later than ten days before the strike, the strike committee submits to the employer, the State Labour Inspection and the Secretary of National Tripartite Cooperation Council the starting time of the strike, its venue, reasons, and demands, the names of the leaders of the strike committee and the resolution of the meeting on the strike announcement.

212. The right to strike is not absolute – Article 116 of the *Satversme* stipulates that the right to strike may be subject to restrictions in the circumstances provided for by law in order to protect the rights of other people, the democratic structure of the state, as well as public safety, welfare and morals.[272] In addition, the employees in 'essential services' have a limited right to strike, which has to be balanced with public interests.

Article 16 of the Strike Law lists the categories of persons who have no right to strike:

– judges;
– public prosecutors;
– police officers;
– firemen;
– border-guards;
– employees of state security institutions;

271. *Ibid.*
272. http://www.satv.tiesa.gov.lv, last visited 15 Dec. 2019.

– warders of imprisonment;
– persons serving in National Armed Forces.

The Law on Bureau of Prevention and Combating of Corruption (Article 13) adds the officials of this bureau as a category of this list.[273]

213. According to Paragraph 3 of Article 17 of the Strike Law if necessary, not later than three days before the commencement of a strike, the employer and the strike committee shall agree in writing and designate from those employees who will participate in the strike a certain number of employees who will perform the work referred to in Paragraph 1 of this Article during the strike, as well as specify the amount of practical work of the employees referred to and give specific orders.[274] The refusal of an employee to perform the practical work and follow the orders referred to in Paragraph 3 of this Article, the aim of which is to ensure the functioning of the relevant service necessary to the public or the minimum necessary work to be performed during strike provided for by the contract of employment or collective agreement shall be regarded as a violation of the work procedures, and the employee shall be held liable in accordance with the procedures prescribed by law. Demands that were not included in the initial strike announcement are illegal. Chapter 23 of the Labour Law envisages the liabilities of employees. Article 86 of the Labour Law provides if an employee does not perform work without justified cause or performs it improperly, or due to other illegal or culpable action has caused damages to the employer, the employee has a duty to compensate the losses caused to the employer.[275] The employee shall be liable only for the reduction of the existing property of the employer, but not for the reduction in expected profit. If losses to an employer have been caused by the malicious intent of the employee or due to his or her illegal, culpable action not related to the performance of the contracted work, the employee should be liable for all losses to the employer. An employee whose work is related to an increased risk of losses shall be liable only if losses to the employer have been caused as a result of malicious intent or gross negligence.

According to Article 87 of the Labour Law, an employee shall be fully or partially released from civil liability for losses caused to an employer if the employer himself or herself – by his or her orders or by failure to ensure appropriate working conditions – is also to blame for the losses.[276] The extent of civil liability of the employee shall be determined depending on the circumstances, especially taking into account the extent to which the balance of the fault has been that of the employee or of the employer. The provisions of Paragraph 1 of this article shall also apply when the employer has not warned the employee of the risk of causing such

273. The Bureau of Prevention and Combating of Corruption http://www.knab.gov.lv, last visited 15 Dec. 2019.
274. http://www.likumi.lv, last visited 31 Dec. 2019.
275. *Ibid.*
276. *Ibid.*

losses, which the employee has not foreseen, and he or she did not have to foresee, as well as when the employer has not taken appropriate care to prevent or reduce losses.

214. Depending on the circumstances, a court may reduce the extent of civil liability of an employee in conformity with his or her financial status.

If losses to an employer have resulted from illegal, culpable action of employees, the liability of each employee shall be determined in conformity with his or her participation in causing the losses and with the degree of his or her fault. Employees who in an employment contract have undertaken the performance of work as joint debtors shall be jointly liable for losses caused to the employer (Article 88 of the Labour Law).[277]

Under Article 89 of the Labour Law, an employee may, wholly or in part, voluntarily compensate for losses caused to an employer. With the consent of the employer, the employee, in order to compensate for losses, may transfer an item of equivalent value or repair the damage.[278] Article 90 of the Labour Law envisages that an employer may give a written reproof or issue a reprimand in writing to an employee for violation of specified working procedures or an employment contract, referring to the circumstances that indicate the violation committed.[279]

Prior to expressing reproof or a reprimand, the employer shall familiarize the employee in writing with the essence of the violation he or she has committed and then request from him or her an explanation in writing regarding the violation committed.

A reproof or a reprimand may be issued not later than within month from the date of detecting the violation, excluding the period of temporary incapacity of the employee as well as the period when the employee is on leave or does not perform work due to other justified cause. Still not later, than within six months from the date the violation was committed. Only one reproof or reprimand may be issued for each violation.

If the circumstances referred to in the reproof or reprimand does not conform to fact or also the circumstances are not such as to suggest a violation of working procedures or the employment contract, the employee has the right to request that such reproof or reprimand be revoked following the procedures specified in the Labour law.

If a new reproof or reprimand has not been issued to the employee within a one-year period from the date of issuing a reproof or reprimand to the employee, the employee shall be regarded as not having been disciplined.

215. The termination of a strike is either voluntary or mandatory. The parties to a collective labour dispute are free to cancel their demands and to end a strike at any stage. Only a court may find a strike or a strike announcement illegal:

– if it establishes a violation of the Strike Law;

---

277. *Ibid.*
278. *Ibid.*
279. *Ibid.*

- if the strike has been announced during the operation of the collective agreement in order to amend provisions of this collective agreement;
- if it is a solidarity strike and does not concern the conclusion or the implementation of a general agreement;
- if the strike is proposed to express political demands, political support or political protest, or if the strike is related to issues, which have already been agreed upon during strike negotiations.

The legal consequences emerging from finding a strike or its announcement illegal are the termination of an ongoing strike or the prohibition to strike if it is not yet commenced. Moreover, if the court has received an application on recognition of the illegality of a strike prior to the date of its commencement, within five days of its announcement, the right to strike is suspended until the final ruling enters into force.

216. Unlike the right to strike, the right to lock-out is not introduced in the Satversme. The right to lock-out was introduced by the Law on Labour Disputes in 2003. A lock-out is the employers' counteraction against employees' right to strike with an aim to protect their economic interests. It is considered as the employers' right to collective action, provided for by the Law on Strikes. Similarly, to strikes, the only limitations to the right to lock-out concern institutions of state and local municipalities as well as essential services determined by Article 17 of the Strike Law.[280]

Article 21(2) of the Labour Disputes Law defines a lock-out as a refusal to employ employees as well as to pay any work remuneration if the strike significantly affects economic activities of an enterprise, providing the number of employees suffering in the result of the lock-out does not exceed the number of striking employees.[281] The decision to lock-out is adopted by an employer himself or by a qualified majority of members of the employers' organization. The indispensable prerequisite of a lock-out action is the submission of the lock-out announcement to respective employees or their representatives as well as to the National Tripartite Co-operation Council and the State Labour Inspection. The latter oversees the monitoring of lock-outs and possesses the right to postpone it for a period of up to three months in case of necessity to take action to prevent natural disasters, large accidents or epidemics or their effects.

Another similarity with strikes undertaken by employees is made by the prerogative of the court to hear cases on finding a lock-out or its announcement illegal following an application submitted within five days from the lock-out announcement. The lock-out or its announcement is found illegal on two occasions:

(1) if it stands in contradiction with the provisions of the Labour Disputes Law,
(2) if it is directed against the exercise of the right to association, thereby violating the fundamental right enshrined in Articles 102 and 108 of the *Satversme*.

280. *Ibid.*
281. *Ibid.*

An illegal lock-out has to be immediately terminated. An additional guarantee of employees' rights is the employers' duty to recover losses of employees made as result of an illegal lock-out.

§2. STATISTICS

217. There are no comprehensive statistics for collective labour conflicts in Latvia, the most reliable data on trends in the industrial relations refer to labour disputes in general. The SLI keeps statistics on submitted written claims without distinguishing them between individual and collective labour disputes. A strike is the ultimate method of resolution of collective disputes that are used in Latvia seldom and usually in the public sector – health care sector and education regarding working salaries and working conditions.[282] There is no information available on a number of lock-outs.

282. The Free Trade Union Confederation of Latvia, http://www.lbas.lv, last visited 15 Dec. 2019.

Chapter 6. Settlement of Industrial Disputes and Protection of Vital Needs

218. The Labour Disputes Law provides for three procedures of peaceful conflict resolution:

(i) Mediation
(ii) Conciliation
(iii) Voluntary arbitration.[283]

The Law emphasizes the role of mutual consultations or parties as to the main instrument for the resolution of collective disputes. In the case of collective dispute, the interested party gives a submission in writing to the other party in which its requirements are specified. The other party must examine it immediately and within a tie period of three days following receipt of the submission has to provide its reply in writing. If the reply to the submission is negative or is not provided, the first party can use one of the methods for collective dispute settlement prescribed by the Labour Disputes Law.

§1. Mediation

219. The mediation is a settlement of a collective interest dispute by inviting a third person as an independent and impartial mediator who helps the parties to the collective interest dispute to settle differences of opinions and to reach an agreement. The mediation method for settlement of collective dispute can be used only upon a mutual agreement of parties. A mediator has a duty to perform necessary activities (including the proposal of recommendations for dispute settlement) to conciliate the parties to the collective dispute and to reach an agreement. Such agreement has to be expressed in writing and it has the validity of a collective agreement.

220. A mediator may be one person or a collegium of mediators consisting of at least three persons. In any matter, the number of persons in a collegium of mediators shall be odd. A chairperson of a collegium of mediators, upon mutual agreement, shall be selected by the representatives of the parties to the collective dispute regarding interests nominated for participation in the collegium of mediators.

A mediator may be any person with the capacity to act if he or she has agreed in writing to be a mediator. A mediator may be private or public. Within the meaning of the Labour Disputes Law, a public mediator is a person (persons) included in the list approved by the National Tripartite Co-operation Council once every two

283. http://www.likumi.lv, last visited 31 Dec. 2019.

years.[284] Each of the social partners shall nominate at least ten candidates for inclusion in the referred to list. Within the meaning of the Labour Disputes Law, a private mediator is a person nominated as a mediator by the parties to a collective dispute regarding interests, but not included in the referred to list.[285]

If the parties to a collective dispute regarding interests cannot agree on a mutually acceptable mediator, each of them shall nominate their preferred private or public mediator and notify the Minister for Welfare. The Minister for Welfare shall select a public mediator for settlement of the relevant dispute who concurrently shall be the chairperson of the relevant collegium of mediators.

§2. Conciliation

221. Collective disputes regarding rights and interests could be settled in a conciliation commission. The parties to the collective dispute shall establish a conciliation commission not later than within a period of three days by authorizing an equal number of representatives. In a matter of a collective dispute, the parties shall write a report regarding the differences of opinions and submit it to the conciliation commission not later than within a period of three days. The conciliation commission shall examine the referred to report and take a decision within a period of seven days following receipt of the report. Minutes shall be taken of conciliation commission meetings. If parties to a collective dispute so agree, the conciliation commission may settle the collective dispute and take a decision following the expiry of the period.

The conciliation commission shall take a decision by agreement of the commission members. The decision shall be binding on both parties to the collective dispute, and it shall have the validity of a collective agreement.

§3. Arbitration

222. If a conciliation commission has not been established or the collective dispute has not been settled in the conciliation commission, any party to a collective rights dispute may apply to civil court. Collective interest disputes that are not settled in a conciliation commission can be resolved either in accordance with the procedures prescribed by the collective agreement or, if such procedures have not been prescribed, through mediation or arbitration.

223. Upon mutual agreement of parties, a collective interest dispute may be transferred to an arbitration court for settlement. The execution of an adjudication of the arbitration court is voluntary. If the parties reach a written agreement regarding the implementation of such adjudication, it has the validity of a collective agreement. During the period when a collective interest dispute is settled in the arbitration

284. *Ibid.*
285. *Ibid.*

court, according to the Labour Disputes Law, the parties to the collective dispute must refrain from exercising the right to collective action, including a strike and a lock-out.[286]

§4. Role of Government

224. The employees in 'essential services' have a limited right to strike, which has to be balanced with public interests. Essential services are defined as services provided by such enterprises, where the termination of work can endanger the state security or security, health or life of society, a group of people or separate individuals (Article 17(1) of the Strike Law). It is the duty of an employer and a strike committee to ensure that minimum work is carried out in essential services during a strike. They must appoint a certain number of employees that will perform the above-mentioned work during the strike as well as determine the amount of work to be done. The refusal to perform such work or to follow instructions is considered to be a violation of the Labour Law. If necessary, an employer and a strike committee also must agree on such activities as the maintenance of an enterprise, its equipment, machinery, etc.

Essential services are defined in Article 17(2) of the Strike Law, as the medical assistance services, public transport services, drinking water supply services, electricity and gas producing and supply services, communication services, air transport monitoring services and services providing meteorological information, services concerning security of transport movement, waste and sewage collection and purification services, radioactive substance and waste keeping, utilization and monitoring services as well as public security services.[287]

225. Article 17 of the Strike Law provides that the employer and the strike committee shall ensure that during a strike, the minimum amount of the work is continued in the services, undertakings (companies), organizations and institutions necessary to public, the discontinuation of which would cause a threat to national security or the safety, health or life of the entire population, certain groups of inhabitants or particular individuals.[288] The services necessary to the public within the meaning of this Law shall also be public transport services.

For example, according to the Paragraph 4 of Article 6 of the Law on Public Transportation Services – a network of routes shall be established to satisfy public demand for public transportation services and to ensure that a network of routes can be used to visit educational institutions, health care institutions, workplaces and state and local government institutions during their normal (generally accepted) working hours.[289]

---

286. *Ibid.*
287. *Ibid.*
288. *Ibid.*
289. http://www.likumi.lv, last visited 31 Dec. 2019.

In the same manner, forming a route network out of cities, at first the possibility for pupils to visit educational institutions should be provided (Paragraph 5 of Article 6 of the Law on Public Transportation Services).[290]

Considering the beforehand mentioned reference contained in Article 17 of the Strike Law, the minimum volume of services that public transport services should ensure, are:

- a network of routes can be used by pupils to visit educational institutions;
- a network of routes can be used to visit health care institutions;
- a network of routes can be used to visit state and local government institutions during their normal (generally accepted) working hours.[291]

226. The SLI is responsible for the supervision of the strike and the lock-out procedures. The SLI has the right to suspend or terminate a strike or lock-out for a period not exceeding three months. It is necessary to take measures for the prevention or elimination of consequences of a natural disaster, major accident or epidemic.

290. *Ibid.*
291. *Ibid.*

Selected Bibliography

Legislation

All documents are published in *Latvijas Vēstnesis* (www.vestnesis.lv). This contains all government laws, decisions, regulations, official announcements, and information about state accession to international agreements and conventions. Until 2013, official state information and legislative acts were published in the official gazette *Latvijas Vēstnesis* (*The Herald of Latvia*' 1993–2012). Starting from 1 January 2013, publishing of the printed gazette was discontinued, and legislation is published only electronically at www.vestnesis.lv.

Legislative acts up to 2010 were published also in *Latvijas Republikas Saeimas un Ministru Kabineta Ziņotājs* (*The Bulletin of the Parliament and the Cabinet of Ministers*). The Bulletin contained all laws, regulations, decisions, official announcements, and information about state accession to international agreements and conventions. Since 2012 the Bulletin has been renamed *Latvijas Republikas Saeimas Ziņotājs* (*The Bulletin of Parliament*) and is published bi-monthly in electronic format only.

Databases

(a) Likumi.lv (http://www.likumi.lv) is legislation in force (laws, regulations), consolidated versions available, Constitutional Court decisions, search mechanism (free of charge, in Latvian and link to English translations), maintained by the '*Latvijas Vēstnesis*'. Provides access to legislative acts and the Constitutional Court decisions.
(b) *Saeima* (http://www.saeima.lv) has a database of draft laws, maintained by the Parliament (*Saeima*).
(c) The Cabinet of Ministers (http://www.mk.gov.lv) have databases maintained by the Cabinet of Ministers: draft legal acts and approved policy documents (in Latvian).
(d) *Latvijas Vestnesis* (http://www.lv.lv) offers an archive of Official Gazette publications (articles, legislation, announcements) since 1995 (search function, possibility to browse issues, in Latvian, requires subscription).
(e) The Constitutional Court of Latvia (http://www.satv.tiesa.gov.lv) has Court decisions, available in English as well.
(f) The Supreme Court of the Republic of Latvia (http://www.at.gov.lv) has court decisions and compilations of court decisions (in Latvian and some in English).

Selected Bibliography

Index

The numbers here refer to paragraph numbers.

Index

www.ingramcontent.com/pod-product-compliance
Lightning Source LLC
Chambersburg PA
CBHW071343230926
51846CB00002B/434
9789403522920